AF412403

THE WORLD BOOK OF
Vegetable, Rice and Pasta Dishes

World Book of Vegetable, Rice and Pasta Dishes

NINA FROUD

PELHAM BOOKS

First published in Great Britain by
PELHAM BOOKS LTD
26 Bloomsbury Street
London, W.C.1
1969

© 1969 *by Nina Froud*

7207 0260 7

Set and printed in Great Britain by
Tonbridge Printers Ltd, Peach Hall Works, Tonbridge, Kent,
in Baskerville ten on eleven point, and bound by
James Burn at Esher, Surrey

To
MICHEL
with love

CONTENTS

List of Abbreviations 8

Oven Temperatures 8

Note on Measurements 8

BASIC PREPARATIONS 9

   Sauces and dressings 9

   Dough and pastry 17

VEGETABLES 19

RICE 56

   General notes on rice 56

   Rice soups 59

   Rice dishes 61

   Rice desserts 93

PASTA DISHES 96

Pasta Desserts 123

Glossary 125

Index 127

LIST OF ABBREVIATIONS

oz – ounce   kg – kilogram
lb – pound   dcl – decilitre (1/10 litre)
grs – grams   ml – millilitre (1/1000 litre)
tbs – tablespoon   tsp teaspoon
opt– optional

OVEN TEMPERATURES

	ELECTRICITY		GAS
	°F	°C	
Cool	225 to 250	107 to 121	0 to $\frac{1}{2}$
Very slow	250 to 275	121 to 135	$\frac{1}{2}$ to 1
Slow	275 to 300	135 to 149	1 to 2
Very moderate	300 to 350	149 to 177	2 to 3
Moderate	375	190	4
Moderately Hot	400	204	5
Hot	425 to 450	218 to 233	6 to 7
Very Hot	475 to 500	246 to 260	8 to 9

NOTES ON MEASUREMENTS

English, Continental, and American weights and measures are given in the recipes. These are not always straight conversions from the English measure, but suitable adjustments. Where, for the sake of convenience, 1 oz is rendered as 30 grams (instead of 28.35), amounts of all ingredients have been proportionately scaled up or down, to ensure that the results are in no way impaired. The cups, tablespoons, and teaspoons, are American Standard.

Basic Preparations, Sauces and Dressings

CLARIFIED BUTTER

Melt the butter on a very low heat until it begins to look like olive oil and a whitish deposit forms on the bottom of the pan. Strain into a clean container and use as directed.

CONCENTRATED FISH STOCK

2 lb (1 kg) bones, heads and trimmings of various fish (whiting, sole, haddock, plaice, etc.)
1 chopped onion
2 oz (60 grs or ¼ cup) mushroom parings (stalks, etc.)
2 sprigs parsley
1 sprig thyme
¼ bay leaf
½ tsp lemon juice
pinch salt
1 pint (½ litre or 2 cups) water
½ pint (2 dcl or 1 cup) dry white wine

Put onion, mushrooms, parings, parsley, thyme and bay leaf in a stock pot. Cover with fish bones and trimmings, add lemon juice, season with salt, moisten with wine and water, bring to the boil, skim then simmer gently for 30 minutes. Strain, and use as directed.

DASHI

The Japanese use *dashi* as the basis for stocks, soups, sauces and dressings. It is very easy to make and the ingredients are available in shops specialising in Oriental produce. The two vital ingredients are *konbu* seaweed and *katsuobushi* – bonito fillets, cut into shavings. In an emergency a light strained fish stock may be used.

¼ oz (7½ grs or 3 tsp) *konbu* seaweed
1 quart (1 litre) water
1¼ oz (35 grs or 5 tbs) *katsuobushi* shavings
¼ tsp Aji-no-Moto (monosodium glutanate)

Put *konbu* seaweed in a pan with water, heat and remove from heat as soon as boiling is established. Add *katsuobushi*, reheat, and remove from heat at the first sign of boiling. Season with Aji-no-Moto, allow to stand for 10 minutes, strain and use as required.

VINDALOO PASTE

5–6 seeded fresh red chillis
½-inch (1¼ cm) slices of fresh
  green ginger
1½ tsp coriander

1 tsp cumin
1–2 cloves garlic
¼ tsp powdered turmeric

Combine all ingredients and pound in a mortar of blend in a liquidiser to make a smooth paste. Use as directed.

GARAM-MASALA

2 oz (60 grs or ½ cup) coriander seeds
2 oz (60 grs or ½ cup) black peppercorns
1½ oz (45 grs or 6 tbs) caraway seeds
½ oz (15 grs or 6 tsp) cloves
20 peeled cardamon seeds
½ oz (15 grs or 2 tbs) ground cinnamon

Mix all ingredients and grind. A coffee grinder does this job very well and the final product should be fine but not reduced to dust. Store in a jar with a well-fitting lid. Garam-masala is an essential ingredient in most curry dishes.

TEMPURA BATTER

4 oz (125 grs or 1 cup) unsifted
  flour

1 egg
½ pint (2½ dcl or 1 cup) cold water

Mix flour, egg and water together, whisking lightly, without trying to make the mixture too smooth. A few lumps won't matter, as tempura batter is intended for immediate use. Never let it stand, and do not allow it to get warm.

AVGOLEMONO SAUCE (EGG AND LEMON) GREEK

2 tbs butter
2 tbs flour
½ pint (2 dcl or 1 cup) hot stock or
  water with a stock cube
3 eggs

juice of 2 lemons
2 tbs cold water
salt
pinch cayenne pepper

Melt butter, add flour, and stir well. Cook for a few minutes, stirring all the time, gradually add stock, stirring to prevent the formation of lumps, keep hot in a *bain-marie* or a pan of hot water. Beat the eggs little by little, whisk lemon juice and water into them.

Very gradually, add hot sauce, stirring all the time to prevent the eggs curdling. Season with salt and cayenne pepper. Re-heat, but on no account allow to come to the boil.

This sauce is served in Greece with many fish, meat and vegetable dishes.

BÉCHAMEL SAUCE

2 oz (60 grs or 4 tbs) butter	$\frac{1}{2}$ tsp salt
2 tbs chopped onion (opt)	6 white peppercorns
2 oz (60 grs or $\frac{1}{2}$ cup) flour	2 sprigs parsley
3 pints ($1\frac{1}{2}$ litre or 6 cups) boiling milk	pinch grated nutmeg (opt)

Heat butter, add onion, cook until soft and transparent. Add flour, cook gently until it turns pale golden, gradually add milk, beating vigorously. Add salt, peppercorns, parsley and nutmeg. Simmer gently for $\frac{1}{2}$ hour, stirring frequently. Cook down by one-third. Strain through a fine sieve. The above quantity will make 2 pints (1 litre or 4 cups) of creamy Béchamel. If the sauce is intended for delicate flavoured foods, omit the onion.

BOLOGNESE SAUCE

6 Servings

3 oz (90 grs or 6 tbs) butter
3 oz (90 grs or 6 tbs) finely chopped cured ham or bacon
1 small finely chopped onion
1 medium sized finely chopped carrot
1 stalk finely chopped celery
8 oz (250 grs or 1 cup) minced beef
3 oz (90 grs or 6 tbs) finely chopped chicken livers (opt)
2-inch (5 cm) long strip lemon peel
pinch nutmeg
2 tbs concentrated tomato paste
salt and pepper
1 gill (1 dcl or $\frac{1}{2}$ cup) white wine
$\frac{1}{2}$ pint (2 dcl or 1 cup) stock or water
2 oz (60 ml or $\frac{1}{4}$ cup) double cream (opt)

Heat half the butter and lightly brown the ham or bacon. Add onion, carrot and celery, cook until browned, stirring frequently. Add more butter and fry the beef, stirring to brown evenly. Add livers, lemon peel and nutmeg. Stir, cook together for 2 minutes. Blend in tomato paste. Taste, season with salt and pepper and add wine. Add stock, stir, bring to the boil, cover and simmer for half an hour. Just before serving, remove lemon peel and stir in cream.

Add the sauce to freshly cooked and drained pasta, mix well and serve. Hand grated Parmesan cheese separately.

CLAM SAUCE (for Spaghetti Alle Vongole)

    2 quarts (2 litres) cockles (or 2 doz shelled little-neck clams)
    4 tbs olive oil
    1 small chopped onion
    2 chopped cloves garlic
    1½ lb peeled, chopped tomatoes (or 1 large tin Italian peeled tomatoes)
    2 tbs chopped parsley
    salt and pepper

Scrub the cockles, rinse thoroughly until no trace of grit remains. Toss in a large pan over a high flame, until they open, remove and discard shells, but strain and keep their juices. Cut into pieces, unless they are very small, in which case leave whole.

Heat oil, lightly fry onion and garlic, add clam juice, tomatoes, parsley, and salt and pepper to taste. Simmer on very low heat for half an hour.

Add the shellfish to the sauce, when your spaghetti is nearly ready. They only need 1 minute – 2 at most – to heat through. If you keep them cooking longer than that, they will become rubbery.

Clams can be bought in tins and need only draining, but they lack all semblance of relation to the sea. If you can't get fresh shellfish, decide on some other sauce for your spaghetti. Clams or cockles pickled in vinegar are too acid and not suitable for this or any other sauce.

CREAM SAUCE

    ½ pint (2 dcl or 1 cup) thick Béchamel sauce (p. 11)
    1 gill (1 dcl or ½ cup) double cream

Add cream to Béchamel, reheat, remove just before boiling point.

HOLLANDAISE SAUCE

    2 dessertspoons water
    pinch salt
    pinch coarse ground mignonette pepper
    3 raw egg yolks
    8 oz (250 grs or 1 cup) clarified butter (p. 9)
    few drops lemon juice

Boil down water with salt and pepper to reduce by half. Remove from direct heat, let the bottom of the pan cool and proceed to cook the sauce in a bain-marie (or in a bowl over a pan of boiling water). Beat the yolks with a teaspoonful of water and add to the seasoned water. Keep the heat very low and whisk the sauce until the yolks thicken to a creamy consistency. Little by little, almost as you would oil for mayonnaise, incorporate clarified melted butter, whisking all the time, until all has been absorbed and the sauce thickens. Remove from heat at once, sharpen with lemon juice and serve hot or cold. If the sauce has to be kept hot, let it stand in a bain-marie; on no account attempt to re-heat it, or it will break up on you.

'Curdled' Hollandaise sauce (which occurs in case of overcooking) can be reconstituted on the same principle as mayonnaise. The rescue operation is similar; start afresh, with a spoonful of water and a clean bowl (or double saucepan), whisking the separated Hollandaise in little by little.

MAYONNAISE

2 fresh egg yolks	$\frac{1}{2}$–$\frac{3}{4}$ pint (2–3 dcl or 1–1$\frac{1}{2}$ cups)
salt and pepper	olive oil
mustard	2 tsp vinegar or lemon juice

Put the yolks in the bowl, season with salt, pepper and mustard to taste. Begin by adding the oil drop by drop, whisking all the time. As the sauce thickens, the oil can be poured in in a thin trickle, so long as you don't let up on whisking or stirring. As the oil is absorbed, thin down from time to time with a few drops of vinegar or lemon juice and continue to stir in oil until all is used up.

MORNAY SAUCE

$\frac{1}{2}$ pint (2 dcl or 1 cup) Béchamel sauce (p. 11)
1 gill (1 dcl or $\frac{1}{2}$ cup) fresh cream
2 oz (60 grs or $\frac{1}{2}$ cup) grated Gruyère or Parmesan cheese
1 oz (30 grs or 2 tbs) butter

Add cream to Béchamel sauce, boiled down to reduce by one-third, stir in cheese and incorporate butter, stirring it in small pieces.

MOUSSELINE SAUCE

Combine $\frac{1}{2}$ pint (2 dcl or 1 cup) Hollandaise sauce (p. 12) with 1 gill (1 dcl or $\frac{1}{2}$ cup) whipped cream.

MUSHROOM SAUCE

4 oz (125 grs or 1$\frac{1}{2}$ cups) sliced mushrooms	1 gill (1 dcl or $\frac{1}{2}$ cup) cream
3 tbs butter	2 tbs Madeira (opt)
2 tbs flour	salt and pepper
$\frac{1}{2}$ pint (2 dcl or 1 cup) stock	1 tsp chopped dill (or parsley)

Toss the mushrooms in 1 tablespoon butter. Melt the rest of the butter, blend in flour, fry this *roux* lightly, without allowing it to colour. Dilute gradually with stock, stirring constantly to ensure smoothness. Simmer for 7–8 minutes. Add mushrooms with their pan juices, stir, add cream, heat almost to boiling point, pour in Madeira, season to taste, sprinkle with dill, simmer, without boiling, for 2 minutes, and serve.

PEANUT OIL AND SOYA SAUCE DRESSING

Heat 1 tablespoon peanut oil with ½ teaspoon soya sauce, mix well and use as directed.

PIZZAIOLA SAUCE

2 cloves chopped garlic
4 tbs olive oil
1½ lbs (750 grs or 3 cups) peeled, ripe tomatoes (or large tin Italian peeled tomatoes)

salt and pepper
2–3 tbs chopped basil or *origano*

Heat the oil and fry the garlic in it until pale golden. Chop the tomatoes, add to pan, cook for 10 minutes. Season to taste, add basil, simmer for 10 minutes stirring from time to time.

This sauce is excellent with steak, fish or pasta dishes.

SATAY SAUCE (I) without oil

4 oz (125 grs or ⅔ cup) roasted peanuts
1 crushed clove garlic
1 sliced onion
2 fresh seeded chillis or ½ tsp chilli powder
½ tsp tamarind (in a piece, if available)
1 tsp sugar
2 tbs lime (or lemon) juice
2 tbs thick coconut milk (p. 16)
2 tbs water
1 tbs soya sauce

Put peanuts, garlic, onion, chillis, tamarind and sugar in a mortar and pound to a paste (or blend in a liquidiser). Incorporate lime juice, then gradually blend in coconut milk. Add water and soya sauce, stir well. Transfer to a saucepan, simmer gently until the sauce thickens.

SATAY SAUCE (II) with oil

2 onions
1–2 tbs peanut oil
3 oz (90 grs or ½ cup) roasted peanuts
½ tsp chilli powder
1–1½ gill (1–1½ dcl or ½–¾ cup) warm water
1 tsp brown sugar
salt
1 tbs soya sauce
juice of ½ lime (or lemon)

Slice one onion and fry in hot oil. Chop the second onion finely, put in a mortar with peanuts and chilli powder and pound to a paste or blend in a liquidiser. Add the paste to the fried onion and fry together for 3 minutes, stirring well. Gradually dilute with water and stir in sugar. Cook for a few minutes to concentrate the sauce to the consistency of single cream. Season with salt to taste, add soya sauce and lime juice, stir and use for basting or serving with all Satay dishes.

TEMPURA SAUCE

½ pint (2 dcl or 1 cup) *dashi* (p. 9)   4 tbs *saké* (or dry sherry)
4 tbs soya sauce   pinch *Aji-no-Moto*

Bring *dashi*, soya sauce and *saké* to the boil, season with *Aji-no-Moto* to taste and serve.

TOMATO SAUCE

4 tbs olive oil   1 tsp chopped basil
1 finely chopped onion   ½ tsp sugar
1 lb (500 grs or 3¼ cups) peeled,   pinch salt
    chopped tomatoes   freshly ground black pepper
pinch pounded garlic

Heat oil, fry onion until it becomes soft, add tomatoes, garlic and basil, simmer slowly for half an hour, stirring from time to time. Add sugar, season with salt and pepper to taste, continue to simmer for 10 minutes.

TOMATO SAUCE, ITALIAN

1 lb (500 grs or 3¼ cups) peeled sliced tomatoes
1 chopped onion
1 chopped carrot
1 chopped stick celery
2 chopped leaves sweet basil (or ⅛ tsp dried basil)
½ tbs finely chopped parsley
salt and pepper

Put tomatoes, onion, carrot, celery, basil and parsley into a saucepan, without adding any liquid. Simmer gently for 1–1½ hours, rub through sieve, season with salt and pepper, and use as required.

VELOUTÉ SAUCE FOR RICE AND FISH COULIBIAC

2 oz (60 grs or ¼ cup) butter   2 oz (60 grs or ½ cup) flour
1 oz (30 grs or 4 tbs) mushrooms   1 pint (½ litre or 2 cups) fish stock
3–4 sprigs parsley   (p. 9)
10 peppercorns   ½ gill (½ dcl or ⅛ cup) cream

Heat butter and cook the mushrooms, with stalks and unpeeled, for 5 minutes. Add parsley and peppercorns and cook for another 3 to 4 minutes on low heat. Blend in flour and cook the *roux* without allowing it to colour. Stir in stock, bring to the boil, stirring with a wooden spoon until the first bubble appears, then reduce to simmering point and cook gently for $1\frac{1}{2}$ hours, skimming from time to time. Strain and continue to stir until the sauce is quite cold. (This prevents formation of skin.) Rinse the mushrooms and use as part of the filling.

VINAIGRETTE SAUCE

Mix three parts oil to one part vinegar, with salt and pepper. Lemon juice may be used instead of vinegar.

WHITE SAUCE

2 oz (60 grs or $\frac{1}{4}$ cup) butter
2 oz (60 grs or $\frac{1}{2}$ cup) flour

1 pint ($\frac{1}{2}$ litre or 2 cups) milk or stock
salt and pepper

Melt the butter over low heat, stir in flour and cook gently for 3 minutes, stirring all the time and without allowing the *roux* to colour. Remove from heat, blend in half the liquid, return to heat and cook, stirring vigorously. When the sauce thickens, add the rest of the liquid. Continue to simmer and beat the sauce until the desired consistency is reached. Season, stir and use at once.

COCONUT MILK (1)

1–2 fresh coconuts water

Have the greengrocer saw the coconuts in half, extract the flesh and soak in enough water to cover for 3 hours, to soften and make them yield up their milk. Squeeze out in a muslin bag two or three times to obtain the amount of milk required.

COCONUT MILK (2)

4 oz (125 grs $1\frac{3}{4}$ cups) grated coconut
$\frac{1}{2}$ pint ($\frac{1}{4}$ litre or 1 cup) hot milk

Put coconut into a bowl, pour milk over it, allow to stand for 10-15 minutes, then stir and strain through a muslin bag, squeezing out as much of the coconut juice as possible.

Dough and Pastry

QUICK BRIOCHE DOUGH FOR COULIBIAC

¼ oz (7½ grs or ½ cake) fresh dry yeast
1 gill (1 dcl or ½ cup) luke warm water
12 oz (375 grs or 3 cups) sifted flour
2 eggs
1 tsp sugar
pinch salt
4 oz (125 grs or 8 tbs) softened butter

Dissolve yeast in water and mix with 1 cup flour to make a soft dough.

Put remaining flour in a bowl, make a well in the middle, put in eggs, sugar, salt and the yeast mixture. Mix and add butter. Beat the dough until smooth and soft. Cover and leave to stand in a warm place for 1–1½ hours. Then use as directed.

QUICK PUFF PASTRY

4 oz (125 grs or ½ cup) butter
8 oz (250 grs or 2 cups) flour
½ tsp salt

4 raw yolks
7 tbs cold water
1 tbs lemon juice

Using a palette knife, cut butter into the flour, add salt, continue to mix, incorporate yolks, water and lemon juice, work with the knife until the paste is smooth, then put on a lightly floured board. Roll out to a thickness of ¼-inch (¾ cm), fold and leave to rest for 10 minutes. Repeat the rolling and folding process three times.

FLAN CASES, BAKED BLIND

½ lb (240 grs or 2 cups) flour
1 oz (30 grs or 2 tbs) sugar
pinch salt

4 oz (125 grs or 8 tbs) butter
iced water (or beaten egg and water)

Sift flour, sugar and salt together – this puts air into them. Rub butter into flour with fingertips, until it looks like fine crumbs. Stir in enough water (or egg and water) to bind and, using a knife, mix to a stiff paste. For savoury flan cases, omit sugar.

Roll out the pastry, line a flan tin, press down gently, to make it fit and prevent formation of bubbles underneath, and crimp the edges. Prick the bottom of the flan all over with a fork, cover with a circle of greaseproof paper, cut to fit the bottom and fill with dried beans or rice. Bake in a hot oven 400°F (Gas 6) for about 30 minutes or until the flan case becomes lightly browned. (The beans can be stored and used again for the same purpose.)

Vegetables

VEGETABLE DISHES

The importance of vegetables in our daily diet is enormous and the variety of vegetable produce infinite.

Most vegetables are edible and some very good indeed in their natural state and various kinds of salads have been dealt with in another book in this series. Here I am concerned with ways of cooking vegetables.

Our markets and shops offer us a splendid choice of excellent vegetables. To appreciate their charm and to do them justice, we must discard the old fashioned way of boiling them to a slow death in 'plenty of water', or of thinking of vegetables as merely an accompaniment to meat, fish or fowl.

Continental cooks, particularly the French who know all about it, have hundreds of ways of preparing vegetables and often serve them as an independent course. In the Far East too, especially in China, vegetables form an essential part of the diet – sometimes several vegetables are eaten daily at every meal and the Chinese cooks have evolved countless ways of preparing them.

Chinese vegetarian cookery is a highly developed art. I remember as a child being taken to a feast at a Buddhist monastery at the end of a pilgrimage. For this occasion the cooks had to create a rigorously apostolic meal with all the appearance of a sumptuous banquet. The meal consisted of twenty-five or thirty dishes, all entirely vegetarian but many of them, probably to make the unconverted visitors feel more at home, were shaped as fish and fowl. The pièce de resistance was a whole roast 'goose' fashioned entirely of soya bean curd. It was absolutely delicious.

The Chinese are most particular about the way their vegetables are cooked and served. They must be just right, very fresh and neither overcooked, nor undercooked. They come to the table with all their colour, juices and crispness preserved. They are never cooked under a lid and never boiled.

Recipes are given in this section for cooking vegetables both as accompaniments to main courses and as dishes in their own right. Not all the dishes are strictly vegetarian. To have made them so would have meant leaving out many great specialities. There is enough choice however from which to compose interesting vegetarian menus.

The recipes included have been collected from many countries with a tradition for good vegetable cooking. Some are designed to provide inspiration for preparing unusual vegetable dishes – either lavish or economical; others are intended to introduce new ways with familiar old vegetables.

ARTICHOKES

Cut off the stalks, pull off hard outer leaves and trim off the leaves with scissors. Shorten them neatly and evenly, cutting off tops to two-thirds of their height. Wash, tie with string around the largest circumference and put, bases downwards, into a saucepan of boiling salted water. Cook, keeping the water boiling, until done. Artichokes must not be overcooked. To ensure this, test the bottom which, when cooked, should 'give' under very light pressure. Drain, dry on a cloth, remove string and serve hot with hollandaise or mousseline sauce, or cold with mayonnaise or vinaigrette (pp. 13, 16).

ARTICHOKE HEARTS WITH SPINACH

2 Servings

4 artichokes
1 oz (30 grs or 2 tbs) butter
8 oz (250 grs) spinach
3 tbs double cream

2 oz (60 grs or ½ cup (grated
  Gruyère cheese
salt and pepper

Cook the artichokes in boiling salted water for about 35 minutes. Drain, remove and discard the inner leaves and chokes, sauté lightly in butter.

Cook the spinach until tender and pass through a sieve or a blender. Add cream, salt and pepper. Fill artichoke hearts with spinach, sprinkle with grated cheese, dot with butter and brown in a moderate oven (375°F, Gas 4).

ARTICHOKE HEARTS WITH EGGS AND CREAM

4 Servings

4 large artichokes
4 tbs chopped *fines herbes*
½ pint (2 dcl or 1 cup) double
  cream

juice of ½ lemon
4 lightly poached eggs
salt and pepper

Cook the artichokes 1 hour in boiling salted water. Drain, cool, and remove the leaves and the choke, leaving only the hearts. Place on a small serving dish.

Combine half the *fines herbes* (parsley, chervil, tarragon) with 2½ tablespoons of cream and the lemon juice. Spoon the mixture into the artichoke hearts.

Place an egg on each artichoke heart. Whip the rest of the cream. Season with salt, pepper, and the rest of the herbs. Heap this on top of the eggs. Chill and serve.

ASPARAGUS

Asparagus is best when freshest. Buy it the day you mean to use it. Snap off tough lower ends, scrape, wash in running water, tie in bundles, cook in salted water until just tender and drain carefully.

ASPARAGUS À LA FLAMANDE

Serve hot with melted butter and halves of hot hard boiled eggs served separately. Let your guests mash the eggs and add them to the melted butter.

Asparagus is also good served with plain melted butter, Hollandaise or Mousseline sauce, mayonnaise mixed with whipped cream, or with Vinaigrette dressing (pp. 12, 13, 16).

ASPARAGUS AND CHEESE CASSEROLE

2 Servings

1 lb (500 grs) asparagus	2 oz (60 grs or 8 tbs) grated cheese
2 tbs butter	(any mild flavoured cheese)
	salt and freshly ground pepper

Cook the asparagus as described until tender. Drain well and cut into bite size pieces. Put a layer of asparagus in a well buttered ovenproof dish. Season, sprinkle with cheese and dot with butter. Continue to fill the dish with asparagus and cheese layers in this manner, finish off with a layer of grated cheese. Scatter tiny pieces of butter all over the surface and bake in the oven, pre-heated to 425°F (Gas 6) to melt the cheese and brown the top.

ASPARAGUS WITH CAPER SAUCE

4 Servings

2 lb (1 kg) asparagus	1–2 tbs finely chopped parsley
3 oz (90 grs or 6 tbs) butter	1 tsp wine vinegar
juice of ½ lemon	salt and pepper
2 tbs drained capers	

Cook the asparagus as described and drain. Arrange on a serving dish and keep hot.

Melt the butter but do not allow it to brown. Remove from heat, add all remaining ingredients, season to taste, stir well and serve with asparagus.

ASPARAGUS QUICHE

4 Servings

Pastry:
10 oz (300 grs or 2½ cups) flour
1 egg
6 tbs oil
½ tsp salt
cold water

Filling:
2 lb (1 kg) asparagus
1 pint (½ litre or 2 cups) double
    cream
4 eggs
salt and pepper

Heap the flour on pastry board. Make a well in the centre and in it put egg, oil and salt and work mixture with fingertips, adding a little cold water when necessary, until you have a smooth ball. Allow to rest several hours before rolling out. Prepare and cook the asparagus (p. 21).

Roll out the pastry and line a flan tin with it. Prick it with a fork on the bottom and sides. Bake in a 425°F (Gas 6) oven for 10 minutes.

Beat the cream and eggs together until thoroughly blended. Season with salt and pepper. Pour the mixture into the partially cooked pastry shell. Bake 10 minutes longer.

Cut off the top 2 inches of the asparagus. Remove the quiche from the oven and stick the asparagus tips into the filling, tip sides up. Put the quicke back into the oven for 5 minutes or until the custard has set. Serve hot.

AUBERGINE CAVIAR

4–6 Servings

2 medium-sized aubergines
1 onion
1 medium-sized peeled tomato
3 tbs olive oil

salt
pepper
lemon juice or vinegar

Bake the aubergines and when soft peel and chop finely. Chop the onion and the tomato. Fry the onion in one tablespoon oil until golden, add tomato, fry together on low heat. Add to aubergines, chop together gently to ensure smoothness of texture, season with salt and pepper to taste, add the remaining oil, heighten with lemon juice, blend well. Replace in the frying pan for 3 or 4 minutes, to evaporate surplus moisture, cool and serve with thin slices of bread and butter.

AUBERGINES SANDWICHED WITH TOMATO

4–6 Servings

2–3 aubergines	2–3 tomatoes
2 tbs olive oil	1 tsp salt
1 carrot	¼ tsp pepper
1 parsnip	tomato *fondue* (p. 52)
1 onion	

Wash the aubergines, cut in thin slices longways, fry each slice in oil and remove. Clean the carrot, parsnip and onion, cut in very thin slices and sauté in the oil in which the aubergines were fried. Add peeled and chopped tomatoes, season with salt and pepper. Sandwich a little of this mixture between each slice of aubergine, place them in an ovenproof dish and press together to make the aubergines appear whole. Cover with *fondue* and bake in the oven for 15–20 minutes at 425°F (218°C, Gas 6).

AUBERGINES WITH ALMOND SAUCE, CATALAN STYLE

4 Servings

8 aubergines	1 peeled, chopped tomato
1½ tsp salt	½ pint (2 dcl or 1 cup) water
4 oz (125 grs or 1 cup) flour	2 oz (60 grs or ⅔ cup) roasted
olive oil	pounded almonds
1 chopped onion	1 tsp sugar

Peel the aubergines and cut lengthwise into slices ½ inch (1¼ cm) thick. Season with salt and leave in a colander for about an hour. Dip in flour and fry in hot olive oil. Heat some olive oil in a saucepan and fry the onion. When it is golden, add tomato and fry together. Pour in sufficient water for the sauce. Add almonds and sugar, check seasoning, adding salt if necessary. Cook for a few moments, add aubergines, cover the pan and simmer gently for half an hour.

FRIED AUBERGINES WITH YOGHURT (PARSEE RECIPE)

4 Servings

2–3 aubergines	½ pint (¼ litre or 1 cup) yoghurt
salt	1–2 cloves pounded garlic (opt)
olive oil	

Wash the aubergines, but do not peel them. Slice, sprinkle with salt and leave for half an hour. Rinse off salt, dry the aubergine slices on a cloth, then sprinkle with fine dry salt and fry in very hot olive oil. There should be quite a lot of oil, at least $\frac{1}{4}$-inch ($\frac{3}{4}$ cm) in the pan. As soon as one side is golden, turn and fry the other side. Drain off surplus oil on kitchen paper and arrange the aubergines on a serving dish. Serve cold.

Stir garlic into yoghurt and either dress the aubergines with it or serve it separately.

IMAM BAYILDI

This delicious way of cooking aubergines comes from Turkey. It tastes even better if prepared and left in its oil for 24 hours. Imam Bayildi means 'The Imam Fainted'. According to an Oriental cookery legend, when aubergines prepared in this way were served to a dignitary of the mosque, he was so overwhelmed by the exquisite fragrance of the dish that he passed right out from sheer gastronomical ecstasy.

    3–4 aubergines
    3–4 large onions
    3–4 (more if liked) finely chopped cloves garlic
    8 oz (250 grs or $3\frac{1}{4}$ cups) peeled and chopped ripe tomatoes
    3–4 tbs chopped parsley
    1–2 tbs currants
    salt and pepper
    olive oil
    pinch thyme
    1 bay leaf
    1 tsp sugar
    water

Cut the aubergines in half lengthwise, without peeling them. Scoop out the inside, leaving a fairly thick shell. Sprinkle the aubergine shells with salt and leave upside down to drain, for 25–30 minutes. Sprinkle the scooped out pulp with salt and leave on a plate. This gets rid of the bitter juice. Slice the onions thinly and mix with garlic, tomatoes and parsley. Dice the aubergine pulp and add to onions. Add currants, season the stuffing. Rinse the aubergine shells, wipe with a cloth and fill with the stuffing.

Arrange stuffed aubergines side by side in a shallow dish, wide enough to take them all in one layer.

Add enough olive oil to cover the aubergines. Sprinkle with thyme, add a bay leaf, cover and cook on low heat for $2\frac{1}{2}$–3 hours. The aubergines should be soft and the sauce reduced. Allow to cool in the sauce, chill and serve cold.

BABY LIMA BEANS

6 Servings

2 lb (1 kg or 1 quart) baby lima
  beans
1 tsp salt
1 onion with clove

2 cloves garlic
1 small carrot
1 small *bouquet garni*

Cover beans with water and bring to a boil with salt, onion stuck with a clove, garlic, carrot and *bouquet garni*. Cover and simmer gently until beans are tender.

BABY LIMA BEANS WITH BACON

6 Servings

1 carrot, quartered
1 onion, quartered
6 slices lean bacon, diced
3 tbs butter
1 pint ($\frac{1}{2}$ litre or 2 cups) water

2 cloves garlic
1 small *bouquet garni*
2 lb (1 kg or 1 quart) shelled lima
beans

Fry carrot, onion and bacon lightly in 1 tablespoon butter, add water, garlic, *bouquet garni* and butter. Bring to a boil, skim, simmer gently for 20 minutes, and add the beans. Simmer gently until tender.

DRIED WHITE BEANS

6 Servings

1$\frac{1}{2}$ lb (750 grs or 3$\frac{3}{8}$ cups) dried
  white beans

2 medium sized onions
salt and pepper

Soak the beans in cold water for 2 hours. Pick over, and wash in several waters. Put in a deep saucepan with plenty of cold water, bring to a boil, skim, season, add onions, cover, and simmer very slowly until tender. Serve beans with one of the white sauces.

WHITE BEANS WITH BUTTER

Cook the beans as described above. Just before serving, add $\frac{1}{4}$ lb (125 grs or $\frac{1}{2}$ cup) butter. Season with salt and freshly ground pepper, sprinkle with chopped parsley, and serve.

RED BEANS À LA BOURGUIGNONNE

6 Servings

1 lb ($\frac{1}{2}$ kg or 2$\frac{1}{4}$ cups) red kidney
  beans
1 pint ($\frac{1}{2}$ litre or 2 cups) water
1 pint ($\frac{1}{2}$ litre or 2 cups) red wine
8 oz (250 grs) unsliced bacon
4 cloves grated garlic

12 small quartered onions
1 medium sized quartered carrot
bouquet garni
salt and pepper
1 tbs chopped parsley

Prepare as dried white beans, but cook the beans in equal parts of water and red wine. Cut bacon into chunks, blanch for 5 minutes, drain, and add to beans, together with garlic, onions, carrot and *bouquet garni*. Bring to a boil, skim, and season. Transfer all ingredients to a casserole, bake in the oven 250°F (Gas ½) for 4 hours.

Before serving sprinkle with parsley.

BROAD BEANS À L'ANCIENNE

6 Servings

1 lb (½ kg or 2 cups) fresh shelled young broad beans	1 sprig savory
4 oz (125 grs or 8 tbs) butter	4 tbs double cream
1 tsp sugar	1 egg yolk
	salt and pepper

Boil the beans 10 minutes in salted water, and drain.

Heat butter in a saucepan. Add sugar, savory, beans, salt, and pepper. Cook covered for 25 minutes.

Remove from heat. Mix cream with egg yolk and stir into the pan. Taste for seasoning and serve.

FRENCH BEANS, BURGUNDY STYLE

4 Servings

2 lb (1 kg) young French beans
5 oz (150 grs or 10 tbs) butter
4 tsp flour
½ pint (¼ litre or 1 cup) hot stock (or water with a bouillon cube)
¼ pint (1 dcl or ½ cup) hot red wine
2 tbs finely chopped parsley and chervil
juice of ½ lemon
salt and pepper

Top and tail the beans and boil them uncovered in salted water for 15 minutes or until tender. Drain thoroughly. Heat half the butter in a pan. Add flour and stir in with a wooden spoon. Stirring constantly, gradually add the stock and wine. Season with salt and pepper and cook slowly until the mixture begins to thicken.

Heat the rest of the butter in a saucepan and put in the beans and the herbs. Cook 5 minutes, shaking the pan occasionally. Add wine sauce to the beans, stirring constantly.

Serve the beans in a heated vegetable dish and sprinkle with the lemon juice.

FRENCH BEANS À LA FRANÇAISE

4 Servings

2 lb (1 kg) French beans	1 tbs sugar
1 lb (½ kg or 2½ cups) tiny onions	*bouquet garni*
2 heads lettuce	salt
4 oz (125 grs or ½ cup) butter	

Trim the beans and, unless they are very small, cut into pieces. Peel the onions but leave them whole. Remove the large outer leaves from the lettuce, leaving the hearts. Wash well. In a deep heavy pan, put 3 oz (90 grs or 6 tbs) butter, all the vegetables, sugar, salt to taste and ¼ pint (1 dcl or ½ cup) cold water. Stir well and bring to a boil. Add *bouquet garni*, cover and simmer very gently for 1 hour. Test. If the vegetables are tender, remove the *bouquet garni*, add the rest of the butter. Check seasoning and serve.

FRENCH BEANS WITH BACON CRUMBLE (OR CHEESE)

3–4 Servings

1½ lb (¾ kg) French beans
salt
12 oz (360 grs) streaky bacon

Top and tail the beans, boil in salted water for 10–12 minutes. Drain and arrange in portions on a heated serving dish and keep warm.

Cut the bacon into strips, fry until golden and crisp, sprinkle over the beans and serve.

To serve as a vegetarian dish, sprinkle with grated Parmesan just before serving.

STRING BEANS ARMENIAN STYLE

4 Servings

1 lb (500 grs) string beans	4 tbs olive oil
2 tbs water	salt and pepper
1 large sliced onion	chopped dill (or parsley)
1 lb (500 grs or 3¼ cups) ripe tomatoes, peeled and quartered	

Wash and string the beans, break into pieces, put in a pan with water, cover with a well fitting lid and cook for 7–8 minutes. Add onion and the rest of ingredients, except dill. Simmer under a lid for 25–30 minutes. Sprinkle with dill and serve.

BEETROOT BURGUNDY STYLE

4 Servings

4 freshly cooked beets	1 tsp sugar
3 tbs butter	pinch grated nutmeg
1 tbs flour	1 clove
6–8 tbs red wine	salt and pepper

Peel the beetroot and grate

Melt butter, stir in flour, cook together to make a light *roux*, Gradually dilute with wine. Add beetroot, sugar, nutmeg and clove. Season to taste with salt and pepper. Simmer over low heat for 10 minutes.

Serve in lettuce cups. Excellent with beef or pork.

BEETROOT WITH ONIONS

4 Servings

4 medium sized freshly cooked beets
3 oz (90 grs or 6 tbs) butter
2 finely chopped onions
salt and freshly ground pepper
1 gill (1 dcl or ½ cup) double cream

Peel and slice the beetroot. Heat the butter and fry onions until soft and transparent. Add beetroot, cover and simmer for 10 minutes. Season to taste. Stir in cream, reheat without allowing it to come to the boil and serve.

BEETROOT IN CREAM

4 Servings

4 cooked sliced beetroot	salt and pepper
1½ oz (45 grs or 3 tbs) butter	paprika
¼ pint (1 dcl or ½ cup) double cream	

Heat the butter until frothy and simmer the beet in it over a low heat for 10 minutes, shaking the saucepan from time to time. Put in a vegetable dish. Heat the cream in the pan without allowing it to boil, and stir with the juices in the pan. Season with salt and pepper and pour over the beetroot. Sprinkle with paprika and serve very hot.

CABBAGE WITH CHESTNUTS, HUNGARIAN STYLE

4 Servings

4 oz (125 grs or ½ cup) chestnuts	1 tbs flour
1 large savoy cabbage	salt and pepper
½ pint (2 dcl or 1 cup) water	2–3 tbs double cream
1½ oz (45 grs or 3 tbs) butter or lard	

Boil the chestnuts until almost tender and peel. Wash and cut cabbage into quarters, then halve each quarter. Put the cabbage portions and the chestnuts in salted water, bring to the boil and simmer until tender. Carefully remove with a perforated spoon on to a serving dish and keep warm. Melt butter, blend in flour, cook on low heat stirring all the time until the mixture is pale golden. Dilute it with the juices left from cooking the cabbage. Season the sauce, stir cream into it, pour over the cabbage and chestnuts and serve.

CABBAGE STUFFED WITH OLIVES AND RICE

4 Servings

1 medium sized cabbage	salt and pepper
2 oz (60 grs or 4½ tbs) rice	1 pint (½ litre or 2 cups) stock
2 eggs	2 sliced carrots
1 oz (30 grs or 2 tbs) finely chopped black olives	2 sliced onions
1 small tin *paté de foie*	pork skin or bacon rind
½ tsp anise seeds	*bouquet garni*

Take off the outer leaves and wash the cabbage, leaving it whole. Cook 15 minutes in boiling salted water and drain well, pressing out all the water. Place on a board and spread open the leaves. Take out the core.

Boil the rice in salted water until just tender. Test it after 8 minutes. As soon as the rice is cooked, drain it and rinse with cold water. Drain thoroughly.

Hard-boil one of the eggs, shell it, and mash with a fork. Mix rice, olives, crushed egg, *pâté* and the anise seeds. Taste for seasoning and bind with raw egg.

Stuff the cabbage with the mixture. Put a little stuffing between each leaf and the rest in the centre. Re-form the cabbage, tie with string.

Melt a little butter in the bottom of a deep pan. Add a wide piece of pork skin or bacon rind that has been boiled 5 minutes. Place the cabbage on this and pour the stock over it. Add carrots and onions, *bouquet garni*, salt and pepper and simmer uncovered for 3 hours, basting the cabbage frequently with the bouillon.

Remove *bouquet garni* and string and serve hot.

RED CABBAGE, FLEMISH STYLE

6–8 Servings

1 red cabbage	1½ oz (45 ml or 3 tbs) water
butter	1½ oz (45 ml or 3 tbs) vinegar
1–2 finely sliced onions	4 cooking apples
pinch salt	lemon juice
freshly ground black pepper	1–2 tbs castor sugar

Wash the cabbage, trim off outside coarse leaves and shred it. Lightly grease an ovenproof dish with butter and put in cabbage and onions in layers, season with salt and pepper, sprinkle with water and vinegar. Bake in the oven set at 350°F (Gas 3) for 1 hour.

Peel and slice apples finely and sprinkle with lemon juice to prevent discolouration. When they are all sliced, add to cabbage, sprinkle with sugar and bake gently for another hour. Stir in a tablespoon of butter and serve.

Excellent with roast pork, goose, duck.

STUFFED CABBAGE LEAVES, RUSSIAN STYLE

6 Servings

    2 medium-sized onions
    4 tbs butter
    1 lb (500 grs or 2 cups) minced beef
    salt and pepper
    1 small cup cooked rice (pp. 56–58)
    ½ pint (2 dcl or 1 cup) stock
    1 large white cabbage (about 1½ lb or 750 grs)
    ¼ lb (125 grs or 1¾ cups) sliced mushrooms
    1 tbs flour
    1 gill (1 dcl or ½ cup) sour cream
    2 tbs tomato purée
    1½ tsp sugar
    juice of half lemon
    1 tbs dill (or parsley)

Chop one onion very finely, fry in half the butter, add meat, season with salt and pepper, and fry together to brown all the meat lightly. Remove, add cooked rice and half the stock (or water with a bouillon cube diluted in it). Mix well, and leave to cool. Dip the cabbage whole into boiling salted water, bring to the boil, remove, carefully separate all the leaves and trim off thick edges to give them a more or less uniform thickness. Put a generous tablespoon of meat on each leaf, fold in the sides, and roll up the leaves. Melt remainder of butter in a frying pan and carefully fry the rolled stuffed cabbage leaves, to brown on all sides. (If you fry the flap side first, they will not unroll. Some people secure them with a thread for frying, but this is an unnecessary bit of 'cheating'.)

Transfer rolls into an ovenproof dish and arrange them neatly, flap side down. Slice remaining onion, and fry in the fat which is left in the frying pan, add mushrooms and fry for 2 to 3 minutes. Sprinkle in flour, add sour cream, tomato purée, stock and salt to taste. Bring to the boil, add sugar, stir, remove from heat, add lemon juice, pour over the stuffed cabbage leaves, and cook in a slow oven 300°F (Gas 2), uncovered, for 30 minutes. Sprinkle with chopped dill, and serve in the same dish.

MARSALA CARROTS

4 Servings

1 lb (500 grs) new carrots scraped and quartered	1 tsp sugar
2–3 tbs butter	4 tbs Marsala
salt and pepper	water
	1 tbs chopped parsley

Toss the carrots in butter in a sauté pan over medium heat to give them an even buttery coating. Season with salt and pepper, sprinkle with sugar, stir and cook for 1 minute. Moisten with Marsala, turning the carrots and spooning the wine over them. Simmer for 5 minutes. Add just enough water to cover, bring to the boil, cover with a well fitting lid and cook until done. Uncover, increase heat to evaporate liquid and leave the carrots nicely glazed. Sprinkle with parsley and serve.

CARROTS À LA VICHY

4 Servings

2 lb (1 kg) carrots	salt
2 oz (60 grs or 4 tbs) butter	1 tbs chopped parsley
2 tbs sugar	

Peel the carrots and cut in thin rounds. Put in a pan with just enough water to cover. Add butter, sugar, and salt. Simmer over very low heat until the water evaporates. There should be nothing but a little syrup in the pan, in which to glaze the carrots evenly.

Season with chopped parsley.

CARROTS, ANDALUSIAN STYLE

4 Servings

1 lb ($\frac{1}{2}$ kg) carrots	nutmeg
1$\frac{1}{2}$ oz (45 grs or 3 tbs) butter	1 egg white, beaten stiff
1 tsp flour	salt
1 tsp brandy	

Wash and peel the carrots and cook them whole in boiling salted water for 30–45 minutes or until tender. Drain and force through a food mill. Add half the butter, flour, brandy, a small pinch of freshly grated nutmeg, and salt. Fold in the beaten egg white. Heat the rest of the butter in a skillet and lightly brown the mixture.

YOUNG CARROTS WITH CREAM

4 Servings

1 large bunch young carrots
2½ oz (75 grs or 5 tbs) butter
¼ pint (1 dcl or ½ cup) double
   cream

salt and pepper
juice of ½ lemon

Scrape the carrots and boil 30–45 minutes in salted water or until tender. Drain well.

Heat butter in a pan and sauté the carrots until golden brown. Add the cream just before serving. Heat but do not boil. Season with salt and pepper and serve very hot, sprinkled with lemon juice.

CARROTS WITH CARAWAY SEEDS, AUSTRIAN STYLE

4 Servings

1 lb (½ kg) carrots
½ pint (¼ litre or 1 cup) water
1½ oz (45 grs or 3 tbs) butter
salt

1 tbs flour
pinch caraway seeds
1 tbs finely chopped parsley

Choose young carrots, scrape and dice. Bring water to the boil, season with salt, put in carrots, cook for 10 minutes and strain, reserving the cooking liquid. Keep the carrots warm, while you prepare the sauce.

Melt butter, blend in flour, cook until the mixture browns lightly, dilute with water left from cooking carrots, adding it little by little and stirring constantly. Add caraway seeds and carrots, check seasoning, stir gently. Sprinkle with parsley and serve.

CARROTS CALIFORNIAN STYLE

6–8 Servings

2 lb (1 kg) carrots
2 oz (60 grs or ¼ cup) butter
salt and pepper

small pinch sugar
1 gill (1 dcl or ½ cup) sherry
1–2 tbs chopped parsley

Scrape and cut the carrots into quarters. Heat the butter and toss the carrots in it to give them all an even coating. Sprinkle with salt, pepper and sugar. Moisten with sherry, cook gently for 5 minutes. Add just enough water to cover. Put on a well fitting lid and simmer for 15 minutes, then begin testing. As soon as the carrots become tender, remove lid, increase heat to medium and cook until most of the liquid evaporates. Sprinkle with parsley. Serve with all ham dishes.

CARROT SOUFFLÉ PIE

2 oz (60 grs or 4 tbs) butter	1 lb (480 grs or 2 cups) cooked,
1 oz (30 grs or 4 tbs) flour	mashed carrots
3 egg yolks	1½ tbs grated onion
salt and pepper	3 egg whites

Melt butter, blend in flour and cook a pale brown *roux*. Remove from heat, cool slightly. Beat yolks lightly, season and stir into *roux*. Add mashed carrots and onion and mix well. Beat whites with a small pinch of salt until stiff and fold into the carrot mixture. Pour into a buttered soufflé dish, lined with oiled greaseproof paper, set in a pan of hot water and bake in the oven 375°F (Gas 4) for 30 minutes. Remove from oven, leave to 'rest' for 5 minutes, turn out on to a warm dish, take off paper band, and slice to serve.

BOILED CAULIFLOWER

1 large cauliflower	salted water

Divide the cauliflower into flowerets and cook them in salted boiling water over low heat for 10 to 13 minutes. Drain, re-shape, into its original form in a vegetable dish. Separately, serve Hollandaise sause, Mousseline, white or cream sauce, or melted butter.

CAULIFLOWER À LA POLONAISE

4–6 Servings

1 large cauliflower	3 tbs white breadcrumbs
4 oz (125 grs or ½ cup) butter	salt
3 hard-boiled egg yolks	pepper
2 tbs chopped parsley	

Boil the cauliflower as described, and drain. Heat half the butter in a pan which should be large enough to take all the flowerets in one layer. As soon as butter begins to sizzle and to take on a light brown colour, put the flowerets in one by one, season with salt and freshly ground pepper, and fry on a lively fire, turning them with a fork, to brown lightly on all sides. Arrange in a serving dish. Chop yolks, or rub through a sieve, mix with parsley, and scatter the mixture over the cauliflower.

Add the rest of the butter to the pan, fry the breadcrumbs until golden, and pour breadcrumbs and butter over the cauliflower.

c

CAULIFLOWER PIE

1 large cauliflower
1 tbs vinegar
6 beaten eggs
1 gill (1 dcl or ½ cup) cream

1 oz (30 grs or 2 tbs) butter
½ tsp salt
Mornay sauce (p. 13)

Trim and wash the cauliflower, boil in salted water with vinegar, drain and rub through a sieve. Add eggs, cream, butter and salt. Mix well, put into a buttered mould and cook in a *bain-marie* (a pan of hot water) until set. Turn out on to a dish, cover with sauce and serve.

SPANISH CAULIFLOWER

1 cauliflower
2 chopped hard-boiled eggs
1 gill (1 dcl or ½ cup) olive oil

2 or 3 cloves chopped garlic
1 tbs chopped parsley

Wash the cauliflower, divide into flowerets, boil in salted water, drain, put on a dish and sprinkle with chopped eggs. Heat oil in a pan, fry garlic and parsley, pour over the cauliflower and serve.

CAULIFLOWER IN SAUTERNE, WITH ALMONDS

4–6 Servings

1 large cauliflower
2 oz (60 grs or ¼ cup) butter
1 oz (30 grs or ¼ cup) flour
½ pint (¼ litre or 1 cup) creamy milk
1 gill (1 dcl or ½ cup) Sauterne or other white wine
1 gill (1 dcl or ½ cup) water
3 oz (90 grs or ½ cup) blanched, slivered almonds
salt and pepper
1 oz (30 grs or ¼ cup) grated cheese

Trim and wash cauliflower, separate into flowerets, cook in boiling salted water for 10 minutes.

While the cauliflower is cooking, prepare sauce. Melt butter and stir in flour. Add milk, wine and water. Cook stirring all the time until the sauce is thick and smooth. Add almonds and season with salt and pepper.

Drain cauliflower carefully, put in a lightly buttered ovenproof dish, pour the sauce over it, sprinkle with cheese and bake in a moderately hot oven 400°F (204°C or Gas 5) for 15 minutes.

CAULIFLOWER LOAF
6 Servings

1 large cauliflower	1½ oz (45 grs or 3 tbs) butter
½ pint (¼ litre or 1 cup) Béchamel Sauce (p. 11)	2 lb (1 kg) peeled tomatoes
	salt and pepper
3 eggs	2 tbs chopped parsley
2 tbs tomato paste	paprika

Wash and trim the cauliflower. Cook in boiling salted water for 15–20 minutes or until tender. Drain thoroughly and pass through a sieve or blender. Mix the cauliflower with Béchamel sauce, season with salt and pepper.

Beat 2 eggs and 1 egg yolk until well blended. Add the eggs and the tomato paste to the cauliflower. Mix well.

Beat the remaining egg white until stiff and fold it into the cauliflower.

Pour into a buttered mould and place in a pan of hot water. Bake 45 minutes at 350° F (Gas 3).

At the same time, heat the butter in a shallow pan over moderate heat. Add the tomatoes cut in pieces, sprinkle with salt, pepper, and chopped parsley. Cook uncovered for 45 minutes.

Unmould the cauliflower on to a heated dish. Strain the sauce over the loaf. Serve very hot. Sprinkle with paprika.

BRAISED CELERY

Trim off the upper green branches. Remove outer stems. Wash carefully, allowing water to run between the stems. Blanch in boiling, salted water for ten minutes. Spread on cloth, open slightly and season with salt on the inside. Put into a well-buttered deep casserole on a foundation of chopped bacon, chopped onions and sliced carrots. Add stock to cover celery. Cover and braise in a slow oven 250°F (Gas ½) for two hours.

CELERY CALIFORNIAN STYLE
3 Servings

1 head celery	4 tbs dry white wine
1 gill (1 dcl or ½ cup) chicken broth	salt and pepper
	2–3 tbs slivered toasted almonds
2 tsp cornflour	

Wash, trim and cut celery stalks into 2-inch (5 cm) pieces. Cook in chicken broth (or water with a stock cube) for 15 minutes. Blend cornflour with wine and add to celery. Continue to cook over low heat until the sauce thickens. Taste, season with salt and pepper. (If the stock cube is used be careful not to over-salt.)

Put into a heated serving dish, sprinkle with slivered almonds and serve.

BRAISED CHICORY

4 Servings

1 lb (½ kg) chicory (US: endive)	pinch fine salt
4 tbs butter	juice half lemon

Trim and wash the chicory. Grease a saucepan with half the butter, put in chicory, sprinkle with salt, scatter the rest of the butter over it in small pieces, and squeeze lemon juice over it. Add 4 tablespoons water, cover with a buttered paper, then with a lid, bring to a boil, and simmer gently for 30 to 35 minutes.

CHICORY À LA BÉCHAMEL

Prepare chicory as described in recipe for Braised Chicory (above). Put the shoots into a warmed serving dish, cover with Béchamel sauce (p. 11) with the juices left in the pan from cooking the chicory incorporated in it, boiled down to concentrate and with 1½ tablespoons butter added.

CHICORY WITH NOISETTE BUTTER

Prepare chicory as described and put in a serving dish. For the quantity stipulated for 4 servings, heat 3 oz (90 grs or 6 tbs) butter over a low flame until it becomes hazelnut brown, *but not burnt*. Pour it off into a heated sauce boat. In the same pan heat the juice of ½ lemon, add to the butter. Stir. Serve piping hot either in a sauceboat or poured over the vegetable.

CHICORY AU GRATIN

Cook chicory in butter as described in recipe for Braised Chicory (above). Arrange in a buttered ovenproof dish, dusted with finely grated cheese. Dust the top with grated cheese and sprinkle with a little melted butter. Brown in the oven.

CUCUMBERS A LA CRÈME

4–6 Servings

4 ridge or 2 long cucumbers	pepper
6 tbs butter	½ pint (¼ litre or 1 cup) cream
salt	

Peel the cucumbers and cut into chunks. Plunge into boiling water and drain. Heat 2 tablespoons butter and sauté the cucumbers to evaporate all liquid. Season with salt and pepper. Cover with scalded cream, and cook until the cream is reduced by half. Remove from heat and incorporate remaining butter. Check seasoning. Serve in a hot vegetable dish.

CUCUMBERS MORNAY
4–6 Servings

8 oz (250 grs) cucumbers	2 tbs butter
salt	1–2 tbs grated cheese
Mornay sauce (p. 13)	

Peel cucumbers and cut in large dice. Drop into salted boiling water and cook for 10–12 minutes. Drain well, mix with the sauce, transfer to a well buttered ovenproof dish, sprinkle with grated cheese, dot with small pieces of butter and put in a hot oven 425°F (Gas 6) to heat through and brown the top.

ENDIVE (U.S. CHICORY) LOAF
4 Servings

1 lb (500 grs) endive	pinch grated nutmeg
3 tbs (45 grs) butter	1 pint (½ litre or 2 cups) stock or
4 tbs (30 grs) flour	water with a bouillon cube
salt and pepper	3 beaten eggs
pinch sugar	Cream sauce (p. 12)

Remove hard or discoloured leaves and cut the rest of the endive from the stump. Wash and drain well. Blanch for 10 minutes in fast boiling salted water. Drain, rinse under the cold tap. Press out surplus moisture and chop the vegetable.

Melt butter in a casserole dish which can be put in the oven, blend in flour, cook the *roux* without allowing it to colour. Add endive, sprinkle with salt, pepper, sugar and nutmeg, little by little stir in stock, bring to the boil on top of the stove, cover and cook gently in the oven 300°F (149°C or Gas 2) for 45–50 minutes. Remove from oven, allow to cool a little, stir in eggs, check seasoning and mix well.

Put the mixture in a buttered mould, stand the mould in pan of hot water (*bain-marie*) and bake in the oven 350°F (177°C or Gas 3) for 20–25 minutes.

Remove from oven, allow to stand for a few minutes, then turn out on to a serving dish, cover with hot cream sauce and serve.

Instead of braising the endive in the oven, it can be simmered on top of the stove, though the slow oven treatment produces better results. By following the above recipe, various other vegetable loaves can be made: aubergine, carrot, spinach, turnip, lettuce, etc. See also recipe for Cauliflower loaf (p. 35).

JERUSALEM ARTICHOKES WITH RICE

4 Servings

½ pint (2 dcl or 1 cup) olive oil
3–4 chopped shallots
8 oz (250 grs or 1½ cups) peeled, quartered tomatoes
2 lb (1 kg) jerusalem artichokes

1½ pints (¾ litre or 3 cups) water
salt and pepper
juice and grated rind of 1 lemon
2 tbs chopped dill

Heat the oil, add shallots and fry until just transparent. Add tomatoes and simmer together for 7–8 minutes.

Peel and slice artichokes, add to shallot and tomato mixture, moisten with ½ cup (120 ml or 8 tbs) water, cover and simmer for ¼ hour. Do not stir, but shake the pan from time to time. Season, add remaining water and simmer gently until artichokes are tender. (The cooking time varies, depending on how young they are.)

Cook the rice separately, as described in recipe for Mushroom Pilaf (p. 77) for 12 minutes, drain and add to artichokes. Sprinkle in lemon juice and rind, check seasoning, simmer uncovered for 5–6 minutes, decant into a serving dish and chill. Serve cold, sprinkled with dill.

BRAISED JERUSALEM ARTICHOKES

4 Servings

2 tbs butter
1 sliced onion
1½ lb (¾ kg) Jerusalem artichokes, peeled, washed and quartered
1 finely chopped clove garlic
salt and pepper
pinch nutmeg
bouquet garni
1 pint (½ litre or 2 cups) stock or water with a stock cube
1 gill (1 dcl or ½ cup) white wine

Heat the butter and fry the onion until soft and pale golden. Add artichokes and garlic. Season with salt, pepper and nutmeg Add *bouquet garni*, pour in stock and wine. Bring to the boil, cover and simmer for 20 minutes. Remove *bouquet garni* before serving.

LEEKS À LA VINAIGRETTE

Trim off the leeks, leaving only the white part. Wash well and put into salted boiling water and cook until tender. Drain and serve with mustard flavoured vinaigrette sauce.

BRAISED LEEKS

4 Servings

2 lb (1 kg) leeks
2½ oz (75 grs or 5 tbs) butter

1½ gills (1½ dcl or ¾ cup) stock or
water with a bouillon cube
salt and pepper

Wash and cut the leeks into chunks.

Heat 2 oz (60 grs or 4 tbs) butter but do not allow to brown. Put in leeks, season and moisten with stock. Cover and simmer on low heat for 40–45 minutes, testing for tenderness from time to time.

Transfer to a serving dish with a perforated spoon and keep hot. Reheat the juices left in the pan, add remaining butter, correct seasoning if necessary, pour over the leeks and serve.

CHINESE LETTUCE I

4 Servings

1 washed cos lettuce
1 gill (1 dcl or ½ cup) chicken
stock
peanut oil

soya sauce
¼ tsp salt
¼ tsp Ve-Tsin

Separate lettuce leaves.

Bring stock to the boil with ½ tablespoon oil, ½ teaspoon soya sauce, salt and Ve-Tsin. Plunge lettuce leaves into it for 30–45 *seconds*. Drain at once, put on a serving dish, dress with peanut oil and soya sauce dressing (p. 14) and serve at once.

CHINESE LETTUCE II

4 Servings

1 Webb's lettuce
1 pint (½ litre or 2 cups) chicken stock, or water with a stock cube
Peanut oil and soya sauce dressing (p. 14)
pinch salt and Ve-Tsin

Separate and wash lettuce leaves.

Bring stock to the boil, drop the lettuce leaves into it, cook for 45 seconds, remove and drain.

Heat peanut and oil dressings, put the lettuce into it, toss to coat with dressing, season with salt and Ve-Tsin and serve.

ZUCCHINI (BABY MARROWS)

Recipe kindly contributed by the Campana restaurant.

6 Servings

2 lb (1 kg) unpeeled baby marrows
3 tbs butter

Neapolitan tomato sauce
2 tbs chopped parsley

Prepare the tomato sauce as described in the recipe for Fettuccine Neapolitan Style (p. 100).

Rinse the marrows in cold water, cut in little round slices, cook gently in butter to soften, add Neapolitan tomato sauce, simmer until tender and serve.

MOUSSAKA

5–6 Servings

5–6 medium-sized aubergines
salt and pepper
olive oil
2 oz (60 grs or $\frac{1}{4}$ cup) butter
1 finely chopped onion
$1\frac{1}{2}$ lb (750 grs or 3 cups) minced beef or veal
4 oz (125 grs or $1\frac{3}{4}$ cups) ripe, peeled, sliced tomatoes
1 tbs chopped parsley
1 gill (1 dcl or $\frac{1}{2}$ cup) red wine
2 oz (60 grs or $\frac{1}{2}$ cup) grated cheese
1 pint ($\frac{1}{2}$ litre or 2 cups) Béchamel sauce (p. 11)
$\frac{1}{2}$ tsp grated nutmeg

Remove stalks from aubergines, slice them, and sprinkle generously with rock salt. Leave to stand for an hour, to draw away bitterness. Rinse, drain, dry on a cloth, and fry in oil to brown both sides. Remove, drain, and keep warm. Heat half the butter, and fry the onion until it becomes soft, add meat, and brown quickly. Add tomatoes and parsley, season to taste, moisten with wine, and simmer gently for 15 to 20 minutes. Remove from heat, add 2 to 3 tablespoons Béchamel sauce, and mix well. Butter an ovenproof dish, line it with aubergine slices, purple side downwards. Proceed to fill the dish with alternate layers of mince and slices of fried aubergine, sprinkling each layer with grated cheese and a few tiny pieces of butter. Press these ingredients well down in the dish. Cover with aubergine skins, purple side up. Flavour Béchamel sauce with nutmeg, pour it over the dish, sprinkle the top with cheese, dot with small pieces of butter, and bake in a moderately hot oven 400°F (Gas 5) for 40 to 45 minutes.

Let the dish stand for a few minutes, then turn out on to a

serving dish and serve. Or serve the moussaka in the same dish as
it comes out of the oven.

MARROW MOUSSAKA

Using zucchini (baby marrows) instead of aubergines, proceed
as described in recipe for Moussaka.

BAKED MUSHROOMS

This makes a delicious course in its own right or as an accompaniment to poultry dishes.

6 Servings

1 doz large mushrooms	2 tbs finely chopped parsley
lemon juice	small clove pounded garlic
2 tbs butter	1–2 tbs finely chopped onion
2 tbs grated cheese	salt and pepper
4 oz (125 grs or $\frac{3}{4}$ cup) bread- crumbs	2–3 tbs sherry

Wash the mushrooms quickly, without allowing them to soak,
dry on a cloth, remove stalks leaving the caps whole. Sprinkle each
cap with a few drops lemon juice.

Chop the stalks and fry in 1 tbs butter. Mix cheese, 3 oz (90 grs
or 8–9 tbs) breadcrumbs, parsley, garlic and onion. Add fried
mushroom stalks, season and stir in sherry. Pile this stuffing into
mushroom caps. Sprinkle the top with remaining breadcrumbs, dot
with tiny pieces of butter, put in a pre-heated moderate oven 350°F
(177°C or Gas 3) for 20 minutes.

CHINESE MUSHROOMS, BAMBOO SHOOTS AND WATER CHESTNUTS

This delicious Chinese vegetable dish, once the mushrooms have
been treated, takes only a few minutes to prepare.

4 Servings

3 Chinese black dried mushrooms
$\frac{1}{2}$ pint (2 dcl or 1 cup) hot stock or water with a stock cube
4 tbs bamboo shoots
4 water chestnuts
1 crushed clove garlic
1 tbs peanut oil
1 small roughly cut onion
$\frac{1}{2}$ tsp salt
$\frac{1}{4}$ tsp freshly ground pepper
$\frac{1}{2}$ tsp Ve-Tsin
$\frac{1}{2}$ tsp soya sauce
1 tsp cornflour
1 tbs cold water

Soak the mushrooms overnight. Bring half the stock to the boil and simmer the mushrooms for 10 minutes. Drain. Remove stalks and slice the mushrooms. Thinly slice the bamboo shoots and the water chestnuts.

Fry garlic in oil until it browns lightly and discard. Toss the onion in the garlic flavoured oil for 10–15 seconds. Add bamboo shoots, water chestnuts and mushrooms. Cook, stirring, for half a minute.

Add remaining stock. Season with salt, pepper, Ve-Tsin and soya sauce. Bring to the boil. Mix cornflour with cold water, blend it into the pan. Cook, stirring, for 2 minutes. Transfer to a heated dish and serve with boiled rice or noodles.

CHINESE MUSHROOMS STUFFED WITH SHRIMPS

4 Servings

8 large field mushrooms	1 tbs finely chopped celery
4 oz (125 grs or ¾ cup) peeled shrimps	¼ tsp ground ginger
	salt and pepper
1 tbs butter	2 tbs oil
4 tbs fresh minced pork	1 tsp soya sauce

Remove stems from mushrooms and wipe caps. Chop shrimps coarsely, toss in butter to warm through, then mix with pork, celery and ginger, season with salt and pepper to taste and fill mushrooms with mixture. Heat oil in pan, put in mushrooms carefully, stuffed side up, sprinkle with soya sauce, cover and simmer for 10 minutes.

MUSHROOMS STUFFED WITH HAM, PARMA STYLE

6 Servings

12 large flat mushrooms	4 tbs finely grated breadcrumbs
1–2 tbs chopped onion	pinch basil and oregano
2½ oz (75 grs or 5 tbs) butter	salt and pepper
8 oz (250 grs or 1 cup) chopped Parma ham	¼ tsp dry mustard
	2–3 tbs grated Parmesam cheese

Remove stalks and leave mushroom caps whole. Chop the stalks and fry lightly in 2 tbs butter with the onion. As soon as the onion becomes soft and transparent, remove from heat, add ham, breadcrumbs, basil, oregano, season with salt and pepper and stir in mustard.

Sauté the mushroom caps gently in the remaining butter, to soften them slightly. Fill with ham stuffing, piling it in a dome, sprinkle with cheese, spoon the butter from the pan over them. Set on a baking sheet and bake in a pre-heated moderate oven 350°F (177°C or Gas 3) for 15 minutes. Serve piping hot.

MUSHROOM PIE LUCERNE

4–6 Servings

Puff pastry (p. 17)
1 lb (480 grs or 7 cups) mushrooms, washed and sliced
4 oz (120 grs or 8 tbs) melted butter
1 tbs chopped parsley
pinch each of chopped chives and marjoram
1 gill (1 dcl or ½ cup) chicken broth
4 tbs dry white wine
salt and pepper

Have the pastry ready for rolling out.

Butter a pie dish, put in mushrooms and mix with the rest of the ingredients.

Roll out the pastry, cover the pie dish, make a hole in the centre to allow steam to escape during baking, brush with yolk or beaten egg seasoned with a pinch of salt and bake in a hot oven for 20 minutes.

ONION OR SOUBISE PURÉE

6 Servings

1½ lb (725 grs) onions
butter
salt
white pepper
½ tsp grated nutmeg

sugar
1 pint (½ litre or 2 cups) Béchamel sauce (p. 11)
1 gill (1 dcl or ½ cup) cream

Slice the onions and blanch in well-salted water for 2 minutes. Drain, put into a pan with 4 oz (125 grs or ½ cup) melted butter, a pinch of salt, sugar and nutmeg. Simmer gently until onions are tender, without allowing them to colour. Mix in thick Béchamel sauce, simmer for 10 minutes, and rub through a fine sieve into another saucepan. Bring to boil, remove from heat, incorporate 2 tablespoons butter, adding it in small pieces. Blend in cream, check seasoning, and serve as a vegetable garnish, or thinned, as a sauce.

SWISS ONION FLAN

6 Servings

Unsweetened short pastry (see Flan cases p. 17)
2 lb (1 kg or 8 cups) sliced onions
3–4 tbs butter
3 eggs
1 gill (1 dcl or ½ cup) single cream
salt and pepper

Prepare the pastry and line a large flan tin but do not bake. Fry the onions in butter over gentle heat until soft and pale golden. Fill the flan case with onions.

Whisk the eggs with cream, salt and pepper and pour into the flan.

Bake for 5 minutes in the oven pre-heated to 425°F (Gas 6), then reduce heat to 350°F (Gas 3) and bake until flan case is cooked and the filling brown on top and just firm to the touch.

BABY ONIONS IN SHERRY AND CREAM

4 Servings

1 lb (½ kg or 2½ cups) peeled baby   2 tbs butter
  onions   pinch nutmeg
salt   3–4 tbs sherry
1 gill (1 dcl or ½ cup) single cream 3–4 tbs dry breadcrumbs
2 tsp cornflour

Parboil the onions in a little salted water for 5 minutes, drain well and put them in a shallow oven proof dish.

Combine cream and cornflour, simmer gently stirring until the sauce thickens. Blend in half the butter adding and stirring it in small pieces. Check seasoning, add a grating of nutmeg and the sherry. Stir, pour the sauce over the onions.

Melt the remaining butter, mix with breadcrumbs and sprinkle over the onions. Bake in a pre-heated oven (350°F (177°C or Gas 3) for 18–20 minutes, to heat through and brown the top. Serve with lamb or mutton.

PEAS WITH SHALLOTS

6 Servings

1½ lb (¾ kg or 3 cups or 2 packets   2 tbs butter
  frozen) shelled peas   1 tsp salt
2 carrots   ½ tsp pepper
½ lb (250 grs or 1½ cups) shallots   stock or water
2 oz (60 grs or ¼ cup) ham

Shell the peas and leave in cold water to prevent wilting while you are peeling and slicing the carrots and the shallots and dicing the ham. Put all these and the drained peas into a pan and fry in butter on a low fire for 12 minutes. Season, add 2 tablespoons of stock or water and simmer until tender.

GRILLED PEPPERS

Choose ripe (yellow or red) peppers. Grill or bake them without any grease, turning them so that they are 'scorched' from all sides. Then, with a knife, scrape off gently the black burnt skin, cut off the stem, cut in half and take out the seeds. Slice and serve dressed with oil and vinegar (or lemon juice). If tinned pimentos are used, they need no cooking at all.

PONT-NEUF POTATOES, OR CHIPS FRENCH STYLE

Peel, wash, and dry potatoes. Cut into slices lengthwise, then into sticks. Put them into a frying basket and plunge into very hot deep fat. Oil is the best fat for frying, but clarified cooking fat can be used. Reduce heat when the potatoes begin to acquire a light golden colour. After 5 minutes, test the potatoes. If they give easily under pressure, remove the frying basket, reheat the fat, plunge the potatoes back into the hot fat to crisp the outside and puff them. Drain and sprinkle with fine salt. Serve at once. These chips should be blonde and slender.

MATCHSTICK POTATOES

Cut the potatoes into little matchsticks. Fry the same way as Pont-Neuf potatoes, but test sooner.

STRAW POTATOES

Cut the potatoes into straws, wash in cold water, soak for 10 minutes, drain, dry on a cloth and fry in hot deep fat. During the first part of the cooking, stir to prevent their sticking to each other. Be careful not to overcook. Straw potatoes should be crisp and golden.

SOUFFLÉ POTATOES

Choose uniform sized potatoes, peel, and cut lengthwise into thin slices. Wash in cold water. Drain and dry on a cloth. For cooking soufflé potatoes, it is essential to have two deep frying pans, one for the first part of the cooking, the other for the puffing-out process. Heat the first pan of deep fat to a temperature of 356°F (180°C), plunge in the potatoes in a frying basket. When the potatoes become golden, but are still soft and begin to float up to the surface, take them out (still in the frying basket). Drain, and immediately plunge into the second pan of smoking hot fat at 374°F (190°C), to insure puffing up.

Drain on a cloth, sprinkle with fine salt and serve immediately.

POTATO PURÉE

6 Servings

2 lb (1 kg) potatoes	salt
4 oz (125 grs or ½ cup) butter	pinch grated nutmeg
milk or cream	

Peel and wash potatoes, cut into thick slices or quarters, and cook in boiling salted water. Do not overcook. Drain. Put in the oven for a few moments to evaporate surplus moisture and, while still hot, rub through a sieve, pressing through with a wooden masher using vertical strokes. (Never sieve the pulp by pressing the masher with a horizontal or circular movement, as this changes the texture and affects the taste.) Put the purée in the top of a double boiler. Set over heat and blend in butter, stirring vigorously with a wooden spoon. Lighten to the desired consistency by adding hot milk or cream a little at a time and stirring until the purée is creamy and light. Add nutmeg, check seasoning, and keep hot until serving.

JIM RILEY'S SARATOGA CREAMED POTATOES

'Put potatoes on to boil, in their skins, in cold water and a little salt; let them cook slowly. When done, set away in the refrigerator for two or three days; do not peel until quite ready to use.

'Have a frying-pan ready with a generous quantity of hot butter in it, and after you have peeled and chopped the potatoes very fine, put them in the pan. Season with salt and black pepper, pour in about half a cup of cream, mix them well, cover for 10 minutes, and serve.'

From May Irwin's *Home Cooking*, The University Press, Cambridge, U.S.A., 1904.

DUCHESS POTATOES

2 lb (1 kg) potatoes	pepper
3 oz (90 grs or 6 tbs) butter	grated nutmeg
salt	2 eggs or 4 egg yolks

Duchess Potatoes are used for preparing various garnishes, croquettes, etc.

Cut the peeled potatoes into thick slices or quarters and boil briskly in salted water. Do not overcook. Rub through a sieve using vertical strokes. Put the purée into a saucepan, dry off for a few moments on the fire, stirring with a wooden spoon. When moisture has evaporated, remove from heat, add butter, salt and pepper to taste, a pinch of nutmeg and eggs or egg yolks. Spread the purée on a buttered baking sheet, dab the surface with a piece of butter to prevent skin forming, then shape as indicated in individual recipes. (This mixture is used for piping borders through a forcing bag, in which case it should be used hot.)

POTATOES DAUPHINOISE

4–6 Servings

1 lb (½ kg) potatoes
1 pint (½ litre or 2 cups) warm milk
1 beaten egg
2 oz (60 grs or 4 tbs) butter
2 oz (60 grs or ½ cup) grated Gruyère cheese
salt
pepper
1 clove garlic

Choose uniform shaped, medium-sized potatoes. Peel and cut in thin slices. Sprinkle with salt, freshly ground pepper and nutmeg. Mix well and put in a bowl.

Beat egg, strain through a fine strainer, and whisk it into warm milk. Sprinkle two-thirds of the cheese on the potatoes, mix, add milk until it just covers the potatoes, mix well and check seasoning.

Rub a gratin dish with garlic, butter it, put in the potatoes, sprinkle with the rest of the grated cheese, scatter a tablespoon butter in tiny pieces over the top, and bake in a slow oven 350°F (177°C, Gas 3), for 30 to 40 minutes, or until done.

POTATO CROQUETTES

Prepare Duchess Potatoes (p. 46). Divide into small pieces, mould into croquettes and roll in flour. Dip in salted, beaten egg with a tablespoon of olive oil added to it, then roll in breadcrumbs, and fry in very hot deep fat. As soon as they acquire a nice golden colour and the outside is crisp, drain on a cloth, and sprinkle with salt.

BAKED POTATOES

Choose large baking potatoes. Wash and dry them, grease lightly, and bake in a hot oven 425°F (218°C, Gas 6) until soft. Cut a cross on top of each, press open, insert a lump of butter, and serve.

STUFFED POTATOES À LA CAMPAGNARDE

Bake potatoes as described. Cut a circular opening on top and keep the cut-out pieces to use as lids for stuffed potatoes. Scoop out the pulp, taking care not to damage the skin. Put into a bowl and mash with butter. Bind with egg yolks, sprinkle with salt, pepper and grated nutmeg, and mix well. For two cups (1 lb or ½ kg) potato pulp allow ¼ lb (120 grs or ½ cup) butter and two egg yolks.

Prepare a meat stuffing, using any left-over cooked meat. Mince the meat and fry with chopped onion, mushrooms, parsley, a peeled, seeded and chopped tomato and a tablespoon of fresh breadcrumbs. Bind with a little gravy and mix with the mashed potato.

Check seasoning, stir and stuff the potatoes with this mixture. Sprinkle the top with breadcrumbs and a little melted butter, replace the cut-out circles as lids, put the potatoes in the oven for a few minutes.

POTATOES AND CABBAGE AU GRATIN, AUSTRIAN STYLE

4 Servings

5–6 medium sized potatoes	2 oz (60 grs or 4 tbs) butter
1 medium sized savoy cabbage	1 gill (1 dcl or ½ cup) cream
salt and pepper	1–2 breadcrumbs
2 sliced hard-boiled eggs	

Boil the potatoes in salted water in their skins, peel and slice. Shred the cabbage and cook for 2–3 minutes in salted water and drain.

Butter an ovenproof dish and arrange potatoes, eggs and cabbage in layers, sprinkling each layer with a little melted butter, cream and salt and pepper to taste. Finish with a layer of cabbage. Sprinkle with breadcrumbs, dot with tiny pieces of butter and put in a pre-heated oven (425°F, Gas 6) for 10–12 minutes to brown the top.

RATATOUILLE

4 Servings

olive oil
1 chopped onion
2 cloves minced garlic
1 peeled, diced aubergine
5 oz (150 grs or 1 cup) peeled, chopped tomatoes
2 pimentos seeded and cut in strips
3–4 small sliced zucchini (baby marrow)
1 tsp sweet basil
lemon juice
salt and pepper

In 2 tablespoons oil, lightly fry the onion and garlic. Fry the aubergine in a separate pan in 4 tablespoons oil until golden on all sides. Combine aubergine with onion and garlic, and add tomatoes, pimentos, zucchini, basil, lemon juice and salt and freshly ground black pepper to taste. Simmer the ratatouille mixture for 25–30 minutes.

Ratatouille can either be served at once piping hot or chilled.

SAUERKRAUT À LA STRASBOURGEOISE

6 Servings

2 lb (1 kg) sauerkraut
1 onion studded with a clove
1 carrot, quartered
1 slice smoked pork or ham
4 oz (125 grs or ½ cup) diced salt pork
4 oz (125 grs) garlic sausage
bouquet garni
4 oz (125 grs or ½ cup) bacon or goose fat
6 bacon slices
stock
salt
pepper
8 frankfurters

Wash sauerkraut in cold water. Drain and press out all the water. Season with freshly ground pepper.

Line a casserole with bacon. Put in half the sauerkraut, spreading it out in an even layer. Add onion, carrot, *bouquet garni*, smoked pork, salt pork, frankfurters and raw garlic sausage. (Prick the sausage in several places with the point of a knife.)

Put in the rest of the sauerkraut, add bacon or goose fat and cover with a layer of bacon. Add enough stock to cover. Bring to a boil, then put in a moderate oven 350°F (Gas 3) and cook for one hour, or until all the meats are cooked. Remove onion, carrot, and *bouquet garni*. Drain the sauerkraut and put on a deep platter. Garnish with the meats, sliced and arranged around the sauerkraut, and with boiled potatoes.

SORREL PURÉE

4 Servings

3 lb (1½ kg) sorrel
3 oz (90 grs or 6 tbs) butter
salt and pepper

pinch grated nutmeg
3 tbs cream

D

Wash sorrel thoroughly, cook in minimum amount of salted water as you would leaf spinach. As soon as it is tender, drain and while still hot rub through a sieve or pass through a food mill.

Melt half the butter, add sorrel, season with salt, pepper and nutmeg to taste. Simmer for 5 minutes. Incorporate the remaining butter, blending it in in small pieces. Stir in cream and serve.

SPINACH TARTS

Tart cases baked blind (p. 17)
1 lb (500 grs) leaf spinach
3 tbs butter
1 gill (1 dcl or $\frac{1}{2}$ cup) cream
salt and pepper
pinch nutmeg

Have the tart cases ready.

Wash spinach, pick it over, discard tough stems, put in a pan with just the water left on the leaves after washing, cover and simmer for 3–4 minutes. Chop, rub through a sieve or pass through a blender. Mix with butter and cream, season with salt, pepper and nutmeg. Blend well, fill the tart cases, put in the oven to heat through and serve.

HONG KONG SPINACH

As in the case of most Chinese vegetable dishes, this recipe has two advantages: all the flavour and the vitamin content of the vegetable is preserved and it takes no more than 5 minutes to cook.

4 Servings

1 lb (500 grs) spinach leaves
1$\frac{1}{2}$ tbs peanut oil
1 crushed clove garlic
4–5 tbs hot chicken stock (or water flavoured with stock cube
$\frac{1}{2}$ tsp salt
$\frac{1}{4}$ tsp pepper
$\frac{1}{4}$ tsp Ve-Tsin
$\frac{1}{2}$ tsp soya sauce
1 tsp cornflour
1 tbs cold water

Wash the spinach leaves thoroughly, drain and shake off surplus moisture.

Heat oil and fry the garlic until pale golden, then discard garlic. Add spinach to the garlic-flavoured oil, scramble for 1 minute.

Add stock, salt, pepper, Ve-Tsin and soya sauce. Stir and simmer for 2 minutes.

Mix cornflour with cold water and blend it into the spinach. Cook for 1–2 minutes, stirring, turn out on to a heated serving dish and serve.

SHERRY FLAVOURED SPINACH MOULD

6 Servings

    1½ lb (750 grs) leaf spinach (or 2 pkts frozen spinach)
    ½ pint (¼ litre or 1 cup) Mornay sauce (p. 11)
    2 tbs sherry
    2 tbs finely chopped lightly fried mushrooms (opt)
    1–2 tsp grated onion
    3 slightly beaten eggs
    1 tbs butter
    salt and pepper
    ¼ tsp grated nutmeg

Prepare the spinach as described in recipe for Spinach Soufflé. (If frozen chopped spinach is used, follow instructions on the packet, but the dish never tastes as good.)

Add spinach, mushrooms, onion and sherry to Mornay sauce. Season to taste. Add nutmeg. Cook together on low heat for a few minutes to amalgamate all ingredients. Remove from heat. Grease 6 custard moulds with butter, pour the mixture into them. Set in a shallow pan of hot water (*bain-marie*) and bake in a moderate oven 350°F (177°C or Gas 3) for 40–45 minutes, or until the mould sets. Remove from oven, allow to stand for 5 minutes, then unmould and serve. This short period of 'resting' makes unmoulding easier.

SPINACH AND MUSHROOM CASSEROLE

4 Servings

    1 lb (500 grs or 2½ cups) cooked chopped spinach (p. 50)
    1 small finely chopped onion
    butter
    salt and pepper

    8 oz (250 grs or 2 cups) button mushrooms
    1 tbs lemon juice
    4 oz (125 grs or 1 cup) grated Cheddar cheese

Prepare the spinach purée.

Fry the onion lightly in 2 tablespoons butter and add to spinach. Season to taste.

Toss the mushrooms in 2 tablespoons butter for 2–3 minutes. Season. Sprinkle with lemon juice and remove from heat. Put the spinach in a thick layer on the bottom of a buttered oven-proof dish. Sprinkle with half the cheese.

Scatter the mushroom to form a second layer. Sprinkle with remaining cheese, dot with little pieces of butter and bake in the oven, pre-heated to 350°F (Gas 3) for 20–25 minutes, to heat through, melt the cheese and brown the top lightly.

BACCHANALIAN SPROUTS

4 Servings

    1 lb ($\frac{1}{2}$ kg or 1 large pkt frozen) sprouts
    1–1$\frac{1}{2}$ gill (1–1$\frac{1}{2}$ dcl or $\frac{1}{2}$–$\frac{3}{4}$ cup) white wine
    8 oz (250 grs or $\frac{3}{4}$ cup) seedless grapes
    1–2 tbs butter
    salt and pepper

This makes a delicious accompaniment to poultry and game of all kinds. Excellent with turkey, venison, wild duck, grouse. For best results, use fresh brussel sprouts, small and firm. Wash well in salted water. Bring to the boil in wine, then simmer on low heat for 6–7 minutes. Do not overcook. Drain, add grapes, carefully blend in butter and season to taste with salt and freshly grated pepper. Heat through and serve at once.

TOMATO FONDUE

    1 medium-sized onion   1 grated clove garlic
    1$\frac{1}{2}$ tbs butter (or oil)   salt and pepper
    $\frac{1}{2}$ lb (250 grs) tomatoes $\frac{1}{2}$ tbs chopped parsley

Chop the onion and cook until it becomes soft and transparent in butter (or oil, depending on whether the dish for which it is intended is cooked with butter or oil). Peel, seed and chop the tomatoes and add to pan. Add garlic, season to taste, simmer gently until all the liquid yielded by the tomatoes evaporates. At the last moment sprinkle with chopped parsley.

STUFFED TOMATOES

Choose medium-sized, ripe tomatoes. Allow two per serving. Cut a circle around the stalk end. Extract juice and seeds. Season with salt and pepper. Set in rows on an oiled baking pan, pour a few drops of oil or melted butter into each tomato, and put into a hot oven 475°F (245°C, Gas 8) for 5 minutes. Make a stuffing with minced left-over meat or sausage and cooked rice, mixed with sautéed chopped mushrooms, sweet peppers, onions, shallots and garlic, or stuff with chopped mushrooms, onion and shallots, sautéed in butter, or with rice and chicken livers. Add the liquid extracted from the tomatoes to the stuffing.

Drain the tomatoes and stuff, piling the stuffing in a dome. Sprinkle with finely grated breadcrumbs and melted butter or oil, and put back in oven until tomatoes are done and top is browned.

GLAZED TURNIPS

4 Servings

1 lb (½ kg) new turnips   1 tsp sugar
¼ lb (125 grs or ½ cup) butter water
pinch salt

Peel the turnips and cut to look like olives. Melt 5 tablespoons butter and sauté the turnips. Season with salt, sprinkle with sugar, and sauté for a few seconds over a high flame to brown them slightly. Add enough water just to come up to their level and simmer gently until the liquid is almost reduced (about 20 minutes).

Remove from heat, add rest of butter, and shake pan to glaze turnips.

STUFFED TURNIPS

Choose round, young turnips. Peel neatly, wash, cut around the base of the stalk, and parboil in salted water for 10 minutes. Drain, and scoop out the pulp, leaving a shell about ½ inch (1¼ cm) thick. Make a purée of the scooped out pulp and cook it gently in butter until soft. Season with salt, rub through a sieve and mix with equal weight of potato purée (p. 46). Stuff the turnips with this mixture, smoothing the top into a dome. Put in a well-buttered dish, sprinkle with melted butter, and bake in a moderate oven (375°F, 190°C or Gas 4) until shells are tender, basting frequently. Allow one or two turnips per serving.

Note: Turnips can also be stuffed with minced beef or chicken, chopped mushrooms, rice and tomatoes, sweet peppers, onions, shallots, etc., mixed with the scooped-out pulp.

DOLMATHES – STUFFED VINE LEAVES

This famous Greek dish relies on the availability of vine leaves – all substitutes, cabbage, lettuce, spinach, lack the pungency and aromatic qualities of vine leaves. Fortunately, when these cannot be had fresh, they are available in tins.

6 Servings

3 dozen vine leaves
boiling water
1½ lb (750 grs) lean veal or lamb
8–10 finely chopped spring onions
3 oz (100 grs or 7 tbs) rice
pinch chopped mint
2 oz (60 grs or ⅓ cup) pine kernels
1 tsp chopped parsley (or dill)
garlic salt
freshly ground black pepper

½ tsp cinnamon
4 tbs olive oil
1 gill (1 dcl or ½ cup) sweet white wine
water
juice of 1 lemon

Wash the vine leaves, put in a pan, pour enough boiling water over them to cover, leave to stand a few minutes to make them pliable, and drain. (If tinned vine leaves are used, they will only need rinsing and draining – no blanching.) Mince the veal very finely and combine with onions, rice, mint, pine kernels, and parsley. Season with garlic salt, pepper, and cinnamon. Add olive oil, and knead the stuffing for 5 minutes. Put one or two leaves shiny side down, place a heaped teaspoon of stuffing on each leaf, fold the stem end first, tuck in sides and roll up neatly and fairly tightly. Put into a lightly greased pan in layers, packing the little rolls closely together. Sprinkle with lemon juice, pour in wine, and add hot water to bring the level of the liquid just below the top layer of dolmathes. Put an inverted plate over them and press it down, to keep them tidily in place. Cover tightly, and simmer gently for 1½ hours. Dolmathes can be served hot or cold. In Greece, if the dolmathes are served hot, they are usually accompanied by Avgolemono sauce (p. 10).

VEGETABLE SOUFFLÉS

Most vegetables make excellent soufflés. Cook lightly, reduce to a fairly stiff purée and dry it out on low heat, stirring to prevent sticking. Mix with a little Béchamel sauce (p. 11), just enough to bind the mixture. Season to taste, remove from heat, stir in yolks and fold in stiffly beaten whites of egg. Bake in the usual way.

The ideal proportion is 3 yolks and 6 beaten whites to 1 lb (250 grs or 2 cups) of vegetable purée. Artichokes, asparagus, aubergines, carrots, celery, courgettes, turnips, cabbage, cauliflower, spinach, chicory, lettuce, sweet corn, tomatoes, with a little grated cheese added to them, or mashed potatoes with finely chopped bacon and mushrooms, all transform successfully into delicious soufflés.

SPINACH SOUFFLÉ

5 Servings

1½ lb (¾ kg) spinach
1 oz (30 grs or 2 tbs) butter
½ pint (¼ litre or 1 cup) thick Béchamel sauce (p. 11)
4 egg yolks, slightly beaten
2 oz (60 grs or ½ cup) grated Gruyère cheese
4 egg whites, beaten stiff
salt and pepper

Trim and wash the spinach very carefully. Boil in salted water for 8 minutes. Drain and leave until lukewarm. Press the spinach between the palms of your hands to extract all the water. Force the spinach through a food mill and put it in a saucepan with the butter. Stir over high heat until all water evaporates and the spinach is quite dry. Make the Béchamel and remove from heat. Stir in egg yolks, spinach, and grated cheese. Season with salt and pepper.

Fold in the egg whites. Pour the mixture into a buttered soufflé dish. Cook 15 minutes at 350°F (Gas 3). Increase heat to 450°F (Gas 7) and cook 10 minutes longer. Serve immediately.

ONION SOUFFLÉ

4 Servings

2 lb (1 kg) onions	salt and pepper
3 oz (90 grs or 6 tbs) butter	nutmeg
½ pint (¼ litre or 1 cup) Béchamel sauce (p. 11)	paprika
	5 egg yolks, slightly beaten
½ pint (¼ litre or 1 cup) cream	5 egg whites, beaten stiff

Peel and slice the onions very finely. Parboil in salted water for 15 minutes. Drain well and put in a saucepan with half the butter. Cook gently until thoroughly cooked. Do not let them brown.

Make a thick Béchamel sauce and combine with the cooked onions. Season with salt, pepper, a dash of both nutmeg and paprika. Cook gently for 10 minutes, stirring constantly. Force the mixture through a strainer.

Melt the rest of the butter and add to the purée, with the cream, egg yolks, and last of all fold in the beaten egg whites. Pour the mixture into a buttered soufflé dish filling the dish ¾ full. Bake 25 to 30 minutes at 400°F (Gas 5).

VEGETABLES STUFFED WITH SOUFFLÉ MIXTURES

All sorts of vegetables: potatoes, aubergines, tomatoes, marrows, pimentos, cucumbers, etc., lend themselves to this treatment. Aubergines and tomatoes are particularly good.

Allow one short aubergines or two medium-sized tomatoes per portion. Cut aubergine in half lengthways (or cut off tops of tomatoes) and scoop out the pulp. Sprinkle with salt and leave scooped out vegetables upside down to drain, while you prepare a fairly thick cheese, chicken, liver, fish, mushroom or any other souffié mixture. Put vegetables right side up in the oven, with a little butter inside each, for 5–6 minutes. Fill with mixture and bake in a slow oven until the soufflé filling rises and is golden.

Rice

RICE

Rice originated in India and China. It was first introduced into Egypt, then into Greece, where it gained popularity as far back as third century BC. It then spread to Portugal, Spain, Italy and America.

Claude Fleury, French ecclesiastical historian and confessor to Louis XV, tried to introduce it into France but the 'graminaceous grain' did not catch on.

Even at the time of the siege in Paris in 1870–1871 when there was a shortage of bread, great quantities of rice remained untouched.

One is tempted to wonder whether this early prejudice is responsible for the fact that the French, with all their culinary genius, have not contributed much to rice cookery, while the Spaniards have their paella and other excellent rice dishes, the Italians have produced risotto, and the Middle East countries have every variety of pilafs.

Rice combines so well with all foods, meat, fish, poultry, game, shell fish and vegetables, that it offers endless possibilities of preparing substantial and interesting dishes. It is a great help whenever the need for economy raises its ugly head, because it can make one small piece of meat or a handful of mushrooms stretch to a respectable meal.

The whiter and more polished the rice, the less vitamins it contains. In affluent societies where it is used as a foundation for other ingredients, it is of no great significance. Anyone who eats rice with meat, fish, vegetables, etc. is not likely to develop any vitamin deficiency. In countries where people depend on rice as their main source of nourishment, unpolished rice is used.

RICE COOKING IN CHINA

Rice, the staple food of the Chinese, occupies roughly the same place in the Chinese scheme of things as bread does, say in France. It is indispensable, but the richer one is, the less one needs of it. The appearance of cooked rice is considered to be of great importance. If cooked correctly, and this is mainly a question of observing the right proportions of rice to water, the grains should be firm and separate. Rice should be washed thoroughly before cooking. Our cook in China used to say 'in nine waters', and the last water poured off should be completely clear.

RICE COOKING IN JAPAN

In Japan, as in China, rice is by far the most indispensible article of food. Rice harvest time is the vital period in the farmers' lives and various colourful festivals in its celebration survive to this day in all parts of Japan. Osaka, for instance, celebrates the Rice-Planting Festival every June 14, when 12 country girls are chosen to perform the ceremony of transplanting rice seedlings in the paddy field of Sumiyoshi Shrine. There are rice-planting and rice harvesting songs.

For ceremonial and festive occasions red rice is often served. Glutinous *mochi* rice is used for this. It is generally cooked with red *azouki* beans and a little red colouring is added to the water. The consistency of this kind of rice takes a little getting used to, but the Japanese love it.

Rice is eaten on all occasions and in all forms: hot and cold, plain and as an accompaniment to dishes of such international fame as *sukiyaki* and *tempura*. One of the most popular Japanese snacks is *sushi*, rice sandwiches, in which cold vinegar-flavoured rice is used in the same way as bread in the West. They can be absolutely delicious or positively revolting and the secret lies in the preparation of the rice.

Rice is used for making cakes and sweets. Japanese *saké* is distilled from rice. Because rice plays such an essential part in the life, economy and diet of the people, great importance is attached to its preparation.

For the discerning Japanese housewife there is no question of getting any old packet of rice and boiling it, just like that. She would know all about its moisture content, which depends upon the length of time since harvesting, and even its place of origin. There is a Japanese standard table for cooking rice, governing the amount of water to be used. The proportion of water to rice varies with the seasons, as follows:

From November to middle of December –
    for 8 cups of rice use 8 cups water
From April to June –
    for 8 cups rice use 8 cups water
From July to September –
    for 8 cups rice use 9 cups water
From end of September to end of October –
    for 8 cups rice use 10 cups water

The measure of 8 cups is the quantity considered adequate to provide a meal for a Japanese family of 10–12 people. This of course does not apply in Western communities. Nor would the standard table be much use to an average housewife, because she is not in the least likely to know exactly where, let alone how long ago, the rice she bought from the supermarket was harvested.

As a rough and ready rule, for those who like to measure ingredients, for Japanese rice dishes allow $1\frac{1}{4}$ cups water to 1 cup rice. There is an alternative method for those who have an accurate eye: shake the rice evenly over the bottom of the pan and add water to reach the level of $1-1\frac{1}{4}$ inches ($2\frac{1}{2}-3$ cm) above the rice. Needless to say, the proportion of water to rice will differ according to the consistency desired.

The Japanese have a special utensil for cooking rice, called *kama*, and the rice is cooked, as is much of the food, on a charcoal burning stove, or *hibachi*. With gas and electric cookers, a thick bottomed saucepan with a lid, or a double saucepan, is best.

Now for the actual method of boiling rice. There are two popular Japanese theories, both of which produce successful results, so it is a matter of individual experimenting to see which you prefer.

An hour before cooking, wash the rice free of all grit and impurities until the water runs clear, and leave in a draining basket. Put in a deep saucepan, add water and proceed as follows:

Method 1: Cover the pan with a lid, bring to the boil over a strong flame, reduce to the lowest possible heat, simmer for 3 minutes, bring to the boil again and lower the heat as the water evaporates. There should be no water left at the end of 18–20 minutes. Bring up the flame to the full for a moment (not longer than a couple of seconds) and remove from heat. Allow to stand for 6–7 minutes and serve.

Method 2: Put covered pan on a high flame, bring to the boil, reduce heat, simmer for 10 minutes, reduce heat to its lowest, simmer for another 10 minutes, turn off heat completely but leave pan to stand for a further 10 minutes before removing cover. Whichever method you choose, bear one thing in mind: never take the lid off the pan while the rice is cooking, because the loss of steam affects the cooking process. You can check how far evaporation has gone (and the rice is ready when all water has been absorbed, so complete evaporation is symptomatic with the end of cooking) by feeling the knob or handle of the saucepan lid. The bubbling of the water produces a vibratory sensation. If you can't feel any 'bubbling' the water has evaporated. It is also important to let the rice 'rest' for about 10 minutes after cooking, without removing the lid. This prevents the rice going gummy and gives it an attractive 'risen' look.

Rice Soups

RICE CONSOMMÉ

Wash rice and cook in stock, allowing half a tablespoon of raw rice per portion. Take care not to overcook – the appearance of the soup will be spoilt if the grains are not separate. Drain and add to well seasoned consommé. Just before serving sprinkle with chopped chervil or parsley.

AVGOLEMONO SOUP

4–6 Servings

3 pints (1½ litre or 6 cups) stock (or water with a bouillon cube)	salt and pepper
3 oz (90 grs or 6 tbs) uncooked rice	3 eggs juice of 1–2 lemons

Bring stock to the boil, throw in rice, season to taste and cook for 15 minutes.

Beat the eggs with lemon juice until frothy, gradually dilute with a cup of hot stock, blending it in slowly. Remove the rice soup from heat, stir in egg and lemon mixture and serve at once. On no account allow the soup to boil after adding the sauce.

CREAM OF RICE SOUP

4 Servings

1¾ pints (1 litre or 4¼ cups) milk	bouquet garni
1 small onion stuck with a clove	1½ oz (45 grs or ¼ cup) ground rice
6–8 peppercorns	½ gill (60 ml or ¼ cup) cream
½ tsp salt	

Reserve 1 gill (120 ml or ½ cup) milk for later use and heat the rest slowly. Add onion, peppercorns, salt and *bouquet garni*. Gently bring to the boil.

Dilute the rice with the reserved cold milk, blend well and stir the mixture into the pan. Reduce heat to low and simmer for 20 minutes.

Strain through a fine strainer into a heated soup tureen, stir in cream and serve.

ITALIAN RICE AND CABBAGE SOUP

6 Servings

    2 tbs butter
    4 oz (125 grs or ½ cup) diced pickled pork
    8 oz (250 grs or 1 cup) peeled, diced tomatoes
    2 tbs chopped parsley
    1 clove garlic
    2 lb (500 grs or 2¾ cups) diced cabbage
    3 pints (1½ litres or 5 cups) beef or chicken stock
    salt and pepper
    8 oz (250 grs or 1 cup) rice
    grated Parmesan cheese

Melt butter, add pork and fry, stirring, for 3–4 minutes. Add tomatoes, parsley and garlic. Stir, cook over low heat for 5–6 minutes. Remove and discard garlic.

Add cabbage, cover and cook over low heat for 20 minutes. Season to taste, add stock, bring to the boil and simmer for 1 hour. Add rice, stir, cover and simmer for 20 minutes. Serve sprinkled with grated cheese.

Rice Dishes

CHINESE BOILED RICE (I)

4 Servings

1 lb ($\frac{1}{2}$ kg or 2 cups and 2 tbs) rice   1$\frac{1}{2}$ pints ($\frac{3}{4}$ litre or 3$\frac{1}{2}$ cups) water

Wash the rice thoroughly until the water is clear. Put the rice and water in a thick saucepan, cover as soon as boiling is established. Leave undisturbed to simmer for 20 minutes.

CHINESE BOILED RICE (II)

4 Servings

8 oz (250 grs or 1 cup and 2 tbs)   water
rice

Put the rice into a fairly broad saucepan and cover with water, allowing 'two fingers' i.e. 1 inch (2$\frac{1}{2}$ cm) of water above the level of the rice. Bring to the boil and allow to boil fast until the water is absorbed.

Cover with a lid, reduce heat to the minimum and leave to simmer for 12 minutes.

CHINESE BOILED RICE (III)

4 Servings

8 oz (250 grs or 1 cup and 2 tbs) rice
16 oz ($\frac{1}{2}$ litre or 2 cups) cold water

Wash the rice several times. Put in a pan, add water, cover and boil over a hot flame until the water evaporates. Do not stir while rice is boiling, as this will prevent the grains from separating.

Keep warm until ready for use, leaving the lid on. (If an electric stove is used, heat may be turned off and pot kept covered on the burner. If the rice is cooked on a gas stove, turn the flame down very low after the water has evaporated.)

CHINESE RICE WITH MUSHROOMS

4 Servings

    8 oz (250 grs or 1 cup and 2 tbs) **rice**
    1 tbs oil (or butter)
    1 tsp salt
    8 oz (250 grs or 3½ cups) sliced mushrooms
    1 tsp cornflour
    2 tbs cold water
    2 oz (60 grs or 4 tbs) sliced meat (lean beef, pork or veal)
    1 tsp soya sauce

Boil the rice as described, adding ½ teaspoon oil and salt. Fry mushrooms lightly in the remaining oil and add cornflour diluted with water. Add meat to the mushrooms. Season with soya sauce, toss together for a few minutes, and pile all these ingredients on top of the rice when the latter has absorbed nearly all the water.

Cover and simmer gently for 15 minutes.

CANTONESE RICE AND STEAMED CHICKEN

4 Servings

    4 oz (125 grs or ½ cup) sliced chicken
    4 oz (125 grs or 1¾ cups) sliced mushrooms
    1 oz (30 grs or 2 tbs) diced celery
    1 oz (30 grs or 2 tbs) diced bamboo shoots
    10 chopped chives
    1 tbs cornflour
    1 tbs soya sauce
    8 oz (250 grs or 1 cup and 2 tbs) rice
    1 tbs butter

Mix chicken and vegetables with cornflour and soya sauce. Boil the rice, and when water is nearly absorbed pile the chicken and vegetables on top of it with the butter. Cover. Simmer gently for 15 minutes. This will be enough to cook the chicken and for it to impart its flavour to the rice.

FRIED RICE, HONG KONG STYLE

4 Servings

    1 tbs lard or oil
    1 lb (½ kg or 2 cups and 4 tbs) cooked rice
    4 oz (125 grs or ¾ cup) cooked peeled prawns
    2 beaten eggs
    3–4 chopped spring onions
    1 tbs soya sauce

Heat lard in pan.

Fry the rice quickly stirring all the time. Stir in prawns. Pour eggs over rice, fry slowly together for 4–5 minutes. Sprinkle with spring onions, season with soya and serve. For Chinese fried rice, it is best to use boiled rice. It has exactly the right consistency.

MOST PRECIOUS RICE

Most Precious Rice (Chow Fan) is so called because it contains an interesting variety of ingredients.

6 Servings

> 8 oz (250 grs or 1 cup) lean pork or chicken
> 8 oz (250 grs or 1 cup) shelled peas (or beans, topped and tailed and sliced)
> 4 oz (125 grs or ¾ cup) peeled prawns (or crab meat)
> 4 oz (125 grs or 1¼ cups) sliced mushrooms
> 1–2 tbs chopped spring onions
> 1 dessertspoon soya sauce
> oil
> 1½–2 lb (750 grs–1 kg or 3–4 cups) cold cooked rice
> 2–3 eggs

See that all ingredients are cut to a uniform size, determining the size and shape by the smallest natural ingredient; thus, if peas are used, the rest of the ingredients must be cut into dice no bigger than a pea.

Beat eggs with soya sauce and keep by. Cook all other ingredients in a deep oiled pan, season to taste, add rice, stirring until it becomes separate and quite hot. Stir to mix well. Pour the eggs over the whole mixture.

Increase heat to cook quickly and keep stirring until the eggs have been integrated into the mixture and are quite dry.

RICE WITH LOBSTER TENDON, TOKYO STYLE

This is a delicious way of serving deep-fried lobster in the *tempura* style.

4 Servings

> oil for deep frying
> 1 lb (½ kg or 2½ cups) lobster, cut
>   in chunks
> *tempura* batter (p. 10)
> 4 cups freshly cooked rice
>
> 4 oz (125 grs or ⅓ cup) grated
>   *daikon* radish
> *tempura* sauce (p. 15)
> pinch grated ginger

Heat oil for deep frying. Dip pieces of lobster in batter, deep fry until crisp and golden, remove, drain quickly, arrange on a mound of steaming rice. Add radish to hot *tempura* sauce, pour over the lobster, sprinkle with ginger and serve at once.

JAPANESE CHESTNUT RICE

6 Servings

3½ cups rice	½ tsp salt
24 chestnuts	1½ tsp *sake* (or sherry)
2 tbs soya sauce	4 cups water

Wash rice thoroughly. Shell chestnuts, peel off the brown skin, cut each chestnut in half and leave to soak in water to soften them. Put rice, chestnuts, soya sauce, salt, *sake* and water into a *kama* (or pan), set on the stove, bring to the boil and keep on a very high flame until rice begins to bubble over. Reduce heat to low, cook for 20 minutes, turn off heat, allow to stand for 10 minutes and serve in individual bowls.

RIJSTAFEL

This is a great Indonesian dish, a vast banquet in itself. Allow yourself and your guests plenty of time to enjoy it, for it is not to be approached as a hasty snack.

The basis is a dish of impeccably boiled rice, used as a canvas for a splendid piece of culinary embroidery. It is the accompanying delicious side dishes, satays and sambals which demand your attention. At a good Java or Bali restaurant there might be as many as 30–40 of these side dishes and each deserves to be sampled.

Most of the side dishes can be prepared in advance and having cooked your Rijstafel you need do no more – nothing, except fruit for the stalwart, could possibly follow it.

Serve cold light beer with the Rijstafel.

All the side dishes are served at the same time, but each on a separate dish. A morsel or spoonful of each is put on each plate on a bed of steaming snowy rice. All the sambals are flavoured with chilli – the amount of which can be increased or reduced, depending on individual taste.

Recipes for the following Rijstafel side dishes are given:

Abon	Vindaloo paste
Tomato sambal	Satay
Fish sambal	Beef satay
Bean sambal	Veal satay
Chicken liver sambal	Chicken satay with peanut butter
Prawn sambal	sauce
Seroendeng	Kemangi
Crispy bananas	Spiced fish fillets
Atjar	Spiced eggs
Lamb vindaloo	Preserved duck eggs

Sweet corn for rijstafel	Beef, Java style
Sojoer	Daging ketjap
Sato ajam	Goreng ati
Chicken and lime	Shredded omelette
Coconut chicken	

SIDE DISHES AND SAMBALS TO ACCOMPANY RIJSTAFEL

ABON

This is a Rijstafel must. Give yourself 24 hours start.

1 lb ($\frac{1}{2}$ kg) lean beef	1 tsp soft brown sugar
1 clove garlic	small pinch ($\frac{1}{8}$ tsp) chopped green
1 onion	ginger (or ground ginger)
small piece tamarind	salt
1 tsp coriander	2–3 tbs peanut oil

Bring the beef to the boil in barely enough water to cover. Simmer until tender, allow to cool and shred. Leave overnight. Grind and pound garlic, onion, tamarind and coriander. Add sugar, ginger and salt. Mix well and rub the mixture into the meat. Leave to impregnate for 3 hours, turning the meat from time to time. Heat the oil and fry the meat until crisp.

TOMATO SAMBAL

3 crushed cloves garlic
small crushed piece ($\frac{1}{2}$ tsp) tamarind
1 small chopped onion
2–3 tbs peanut oil
2 fresh seeded and shredded red chillies
1 lb ($\frac{1}{2}$ kg or 2 cups) fresh, peeled and sliced tomatoes
1–2 well washed, sliced leeks
salt
1 tbs brown sugar
1 gill (1 dcl or $\frac{1}{2}$ cup) coconut milk (p. 16)

Fry garlic, tamarind and onion in oil for 3–4 minutes. Add chillies and tomatoes. Cook, stirring, for 2 minutes. Add leeks, stir and cook for 2 minutes. Sprinkle with salt and sugar. Gradually blend in coconut milk, bring to the boil, simmer gently for 10 minutes and serve.

FISH SAMBAL

3 cloves garlic
2 seeded fresh red chillis (or 1 tsp chilli powder)
$\frac{1}{2}$ tsp cumin seed
$\frac{1}{4}$ tsp turmeric
1 seeded, sliced green pepper

E

1 large finely sliced onion
1-inch (2½ cm) piece finely chopped root ginger
2–3 tbs peanut oil
1 lb (500 grs) fish (any firm white fish) boiled, skinned and boned
salt
½ pint (2 dcl or 1 cup) coconut milk (p. 16)

Pound together in a mortar or blend in a liquidiser the garlic, chillis, cumin and turmeric until they form a smooth paste. Heat oil and fry green pepper, onion and ginger for 2 minutes. Add spice paste and stir quickly. Add fish, which should be lightly boiled (not overcooked) and cut into portions. Cook gently to heat the fish and permeate it by the spices, for 2–3 minutes. Season with salt to taste. Add coconut milk, simmer for 5–6 minutes.

BEAN SAMBAL

1 small onion
1–2 cloves garlic
2 fresh seeded red chillis
small piece (½ tsp) tamarind
2–3 tbs peanut oil
1 lb (½ kg) French beans

1 tsp brown sugar
salt
1 small bay leaf
1 dried lemon leaf
½ pint (2 dcl or 1 cup) coconut milk (p. 16)

Pound together, or blend in a liquidiser, onion, garlic, chillis and tamarind until they are reduced to a smooth paste. Fry in oil for 5 minutes.

Top and tail the beans, shred and add to spice paste. Stir well. Add sugar, salt to taste, bay and lemon leaf. Gradually blend in coconut milk. Bring to the boil, then simmer uncovered for 10–12 minutes.

CHICKEN LIVER SAMBAL

1 chopped onion
1 clove garlic
½ tsp tamarind (in a piece if possible)
1–2 fresh seeded chillis
2–3 tbs peanut oil
1 lb (½ kg) chicken livers
½ tsp powdered ginger
1 tsp brown sugar
pinch salt
12 oz (360 ml or 1½ cups) coconut milk (p. 16)

Pound together or blend in a liquidiser onion, garlic, tamarind and the chillis into a smooth paste. Fry in oil for 5 minutes. Cut livers into bite-size pieces, add to fried spices, sprinkle with ginger and sugar, season with salt to taste and fry lightly stirring all the time to mix well. Add coconut milk, blending it in a little at a time. Simmer until the sauce thickens.

PRAWN SAMBAL

As Chicken Liver sambal, substituting equivalent amount of
peeled prawns for liver.

SEROENDENG

This is a coconut condiment, a small helping of which is served
with Rijstafel, along with dishes of various *ATJAR* or vegetable pickles.

    1 chopped onion
    1–2 crushed cloves garlic
    1-inch piece chopped root ginger
    1 small bay leaf
    1 dried lemon leaf
    1 tsp coriander
    ½ tsp cumin seed
    8 oz (250 grs or 3 cups) shredded coconut
    2–3 tbs water
    salt
    1 tsp soft brown sugar
    4 oz (125 grs or ⅔ cup) lightly roasted peanuts

Pound together or blend in a liquidiser the onion, garlic, ginger,
bay leaf, lemon leaf, coriander and cumin. Quickly dry-fry (i.e.
without any fat) this spice paste to brown lightly.

In a separate pan, dry-fry coconut, to brown lightly. Add spice
paste, dilute with a little water, season with salt to taste, sprinkle
with sugar and cook together for 3–4 minutes. Add peanuts and serve.

CRISPY BANANAS

    peanut oil for deep frying   lemon juice
    3–4 ripe bananas   2–3 tbs brown sugar

Heat the oil. Peel and cut bananas in half lengthwise, dip in
lemon juice, coat with brown sugar and fry until crisp and golden.
Drain on tissue paper and serve at once.

ATJAR (vegetable pickle for Rijstafel)

    1 finely sliced carrot
    2 seeded, finely sliced green peppers
    1 finely sliced cucumber
    4 oz (125 grs or ½ cup) sliced runner beans
    ½ lb (250 grs or 1 cup) peeled shallots
    water
    salt
    4–5 blanched cadjunuts or almonds
    1 tsp turmeric
    2 cloves garlic
    1-inch (2½ cm) slice of fresh green ginger
    1 pint (½ litre or 2 cups) vinegar
    1–1½ tbs brown sugar

Drop the carrot, peppers, cucumbers, beans and shallots into enough salted boiling water to cover, cook for 4–5 minutes and drain well.

Pound in a mortar the nuts, turmeric, garlic and ginger, or blend in a liquidiser, to reduce them to a smooth paste. Gradually dilute with vinegar and 1 gill (1 dcl or ½ cup) water. Season with salt to taste. Add sugar, mix well and bring to the boil. Add parboiled vegetables, cook for 10 minutes. Allow to cool then chill. Serve cold.

LAMB VINDALOO

1½ lb (1¼ kg) lean lamb	1 gill (1 dcl or ½ cup) vinegar
Vindaloo paste (p. 10)	water
salt	

Trim and cut the meat into bite-size pieces. Blend with vindaloo paste, season with salt to taste, add vinegar, mix well and leave to macerate for 1–2 hours. Fry without adding any fat, but moistening with a few tablespoons of water, as required. Stir frequently. As soon as the lamb is tender, serve.

SATAY

This is an Indonesian speciality, but is also popular in parts of South China and Malaya. Street vendors in Java sell them the way hot dogs are sold in America, but the satay are much more tempting.

It is a variation on all the kebabs. The meat is cut into bite-size cubes, steeped in a special marinade, almost always containing creamy coconut milk (p. 16), threaded on small bamboo or palm leaf skewers, grilled and served with Satay sauce (p. 14).

Satay can be made of beef, veal, pork, any kind of poultry meat, chicken livers, etc.

5–6 pieces of meat are threaded on one skewer and 2 skewers usually allowed per portion.

Skewers of piping hot Satay, with a bowl of Satay sauce handed separately, make splendid cocktail food.

VEAL SATAY

4 Servings

1 lb (½ kg) veal	½ pint (2 dcl or 1 cup) coconut
1 tbs almonds	milk (p. 16)
1 sliced piece of root ginger	salt and pepper
1 tsp coriander	1 tsp brown sugar
1 tsp turmeric	

Pound the almonds, ginger, coriander, and turmeric, to a paste, gradually dilute with coconut milk. Cut the veal into bite-size cubes, season to taste with salt and freshly ground pepper, put into spiced coconut milk, and leave to marinate for 2 hours. Remove pieces of veal, impale on skewers, sprinkle with sugar, and grill, turning and basting frequently with the coconut liquid. Serve with Satay sauce (p. 14).

BEEF SATAY

Follow recipe for Veal Satay, substituting fillet of beef for veal. Allow 4–5 pieces of beef to each skewer, grill turning often and basting with the marinading liquid. Dip in Satay sauce (p. 14) just before serving. Serve the rest of the sauce separately.

CHICKEN SATAY WITH PEANUT BUTTER SAUCE

1 roasting chicken
1½ tsp salt
freshly ground black pepper
1 gill (1 dcl or ½ cup) creamy coconut milk (p. 16)
3–4 tbs peanut butter
1 tsp chilli powder
1 tsp grated lemon rind
1½ tsp brown sugar
12 oz (360 ml or 1½ cups) hot water
juice of ½ lime (or lemon)

Cut the chicken into 1-inch (2½ cm) pieces.

Combine salt, pepper and coconut milk in a dish, put the chicken into it and leave to marinade for 1–2 hours. Skewer and grill as described, basting with the marinade. Put peanut butter, chilli powder, lemon rind, sugar and water into a saucepan, bring to the boil, then reduce heat and simmer for 15 minutes. Remove from heat, stir in lime juice, spoon a little over each skewer and serve the rest in a sauce boat.

KEMANGI

Kemangi are obviously of European origin, probably Dutch, but have become a classic Rijstafel side dish.

They can be made of any good cooked, but not overcooked, meat: beef, veal, pork, or chicken. They are delicious made of ham, or prawns or mushrooms. More than one kind of Kemangi is sometimes served at a Rijstafel meal.

8 oz (250 grs or 1 cup) cooked
  meat or chicken
white sauce (p. 16)
salt and pepper
juice of ½ lime (or lemon)

1½ tsp chopped parsley
peanut oil for deep frying
flour
1–2 beaten eggs
breadcrumbs

Mince the meat. Prepare white sauce. When it thickens, check seasoning and stir in lime juice. Remove from heat, add meat and parsley, mix well and spread the Kemangi mixture on a shallow dish to cool.

Put oil to heat.

Taking a teaspoon of the mixture, shape into little balls, roll in flour, dip in beaten egg, coat with breadcrumbs and deepfry until golden. Drain on tissue paper and serve with Satay sauce (p. 14) in a separate sauce boat. The above amount should make 20–25 Kemangi.

SPICED FISH FILLETS

1 lb (500 grs) fish fillets (mullet for preference)
walnut-size piece of tamarind
3–4 tbs peanut oil
2 finely chopped onions
2 finely chopped cloves garlic

½ tsp fresh chillis (opt)
1 tbs soya sauce
2 tbs water
1 tsp soft brown sugar
juice of 1 lime (or lemon)

Rub the fish fillets with tamarind, then fry them in hot oil to brown both sides. Reduce heat, add onions and garlic and cook for 3–4 minutes. Add chilli and fry lightly. Mix soya sauce, water, sugar and lime juice and pour over the fish. Bring to the boil, simmer for 3–4 *seconds* and serve.

PRESERVED DUCK EGGS

This is a Chinese delicacy and an essential part of Rijstafel. In China they are preserved in a solution of salt, lime and soda or potash. They can be bought ready for use in Chinese food shops. In Java they are dipped in salt water solution, dried and buried in a flower pot for anything from 10–30 days. Hardboil and cut in half before serving.

SPICED EGGS

4 eggs
½ pint (2 dcl or 1 cup) coconut milk (p. 16)
1½ tbs chopped onion
1 chopped clove garlic

1 tbs grated fresh ginger
1 tsp cumin seed
1 tsp coriander
1½ tbs peanut oil

Put the eggs into enough cold water to cover, bring to the boil. As soon as boiling is established, cover the pan, turn off heat and leave for 15 minutes. Then, dip in cold water, shell and cut in half. Prepare coconut milk as described, making it fairly thick. Pound the onion, garlic, ginger, cumin and coriander into a smooth mixture (or blend in a liquidiser). Heat the oil and fry the pounded spices for 5–6 minutes stirring all the time. Dilute gradually with coconut milk, add eggs, simmer gently without a lid for 10–12 minutes and serve.

SWEET CORN FOR RIJSTAFEL

Oil for deep frying
8 oz (250 grs or 1 cup) cooked whole corn kernels (boiled and scraped off the cob, or 1 tin sweet corn)
1 tbs chopped celery
1 tbs finely chopped shallot
1 finely chopped clove garlic
1 tbs chopped parsley
$\frac{1}{2}$ tsp salt
$\frac{1}{4}$ tsp freshly ground pepper
1–2 beaten eggs (depending on size)
1–2 tbs flour

Put the oil to heat. Combine all ingredients and taking a spoonful at a time drop into hot oil. Fry until golden on both sides and crisp on the outside.

SAJOER

This is an Indonesian soup which forms a part of the Rijstafel menu. It can be served in individual bowl or spooned over boiled rice.

8 Servings

2 chopped onions
2 cloves crushed garlic
1 tsp cumin seed
1 tsp coriander
1 tsp fresh sliced ginger
$\frac{1}{2}$ tsp chilli powder
1 bayleaf
1 dried lemon leaf
2 tsp salt
2 tbs peanut oil
3 pints (1$\frac{1}{2}$ litre or 6 cups) coconut milk (p. 16)
1 shredded carrot
4 oz (125 grs or $\frac{1}{3}$ cup) sliced runner beans
6 oz (180 grs or $\frac{1}{2}$ cup) shredded cabbage or Brussel sprouts
4 oz (125 grs or $\frac{1}{3}$ cup) peas
small cauliflower, divided into flowerets
1 oz (250 grs or 1 cup) finely minced lean beef
1 tsp grated lemon rind
1 sweet pepper, seeded and cut in shreds
1 tsp paprika
pinch brown sugar
1 finely sliced onion
3–4 tbs grated coconut
8 oz (250 grs or 1 cup) peeled prawns

Blend in a liquidiser or pound in a mortar chopped onions, garlic, cumin, coriander, ginger, chilli, bayleaf, lemon leaf and a teaspoon salt until all these ingredients are reduced to a smooth paste. Cook it for 3 minutes in hot oil, stirring constantly. Dilute with coconut milk, blend well and bring to the boil. Add carrot, beans, cabbage, peas, cauliflower, beef, lemon rind and pepper. Season with salt and paprika, sprinkle with sugar. Cook over low heat for 15–20 minutes and make sure you have enough coconut milk to prevent drying out.

Fry the sliced onion in oil until very crisp.

Transfer Sajoer into a serving bowl, garnish with prawns, fried onion and grated coconut and serve.

SOTO AJAM (Chicken and vermicelli)

1 boiling fowl	1 onion
1 tsp turmeric	1–2 tbs peanut oil
1 inch (2½ cm) piece of green ginger	2 oz (60 grs) Chinese vermicelli
	salt
2–3 cloves garlic	10–12 chopped spring onions

Simmer the chicken in salted water to cover until tender. Drain and bone the chicken, leaving the stock meanwhile to boil down by half, to concentrate it. Drop the bones back into the stock as you take the chicken meat off them.

Pound the turmeric, ginger and onion, with a pinch of salt in a mortar (or reduce to paste in a blender). Fry the mixture in oil for 3 minutes.

Strain the stock, add chicken, stir in spice paste, bring to the boil, simmer for 10 minutes uncovered.

Add Chinese vermicelli and boil fast for 5 minutes. Check seasoning and add salt, if necessary. Sprinkle with spring onions, cook for 5 minutes and serve.

CHICKEN AND LIME

1 roasting chicken, cut in portions	¼ tsp powdered turmeric
4–5 tbs oil	½–1 tsp chilli powder
1–2 pounded cloves garlic	1–1½ tbs soya sauce
1 tsp finely chopped onion	salt and pepper
½ tsp coriander	2–3 fresh limes
½ tsp ground cumin seed	

Trim the chicken pieces neatly and brown in oil. Remove. In the same pan fry garlic and onion until soft. Add coriander, cumin, turmeric, chilli powder, soya sauce and salt and pepper to taste. Mix well, cook together on low heat for 1–2 minutes. Add chicken, check seasoning, add more salt if necessary. Spoon the juices over the chicken and cook gently until tender. Squeeze the juice of 1 lime and sprinkle over the chicken. Stir, add the remaining limes cut into segments, cook for 3–4 minutes, spooning the sauce over the chicken and serve.

COCONUT CHICKEN

2 coconuts
1 finely sliced onion
1 chopped clove garlic
2 tbs oil
12 oz (360 grs or 1½ cups) cooked
    diced chicken

¼ tsp chilli powder
1 tsp fresh grated ginger
1–2 tsp ground coriander
salt

Using 1½ coconuts, extract 1 pint (½ litre or 2 cups) coconut milk as described on p. 16. Shred the remaining half coconut. Fry the onion, garlic and shredded coconut in oil. Remove from heat and transfer to a casserole. Add chicken, chilli, ginger, coriander, coconut milk and salt to taste. Mix well. Bring to the boil, reduce heat, simmer uncovered gently for 15–20 minutes.

BEEF FOR RIJSTAFEL, JAVA STYLE

4 Servings

1 lb (½ kg) steak
2 tbs peanut oil
2 medium-sized onions
1 grated clove garlic

salt
small pinch chilli powder
1 gill (1 dcl or ½ cup) coconut milk
(p. 16)

Cut the meat into bite-size pieces and brown lightly in oil. Chop onions, and add to pan with garlic, salt and chilli powder. Mix well, and cook until onions turn pale golden. Add coconut milk, stir, simmer for 15 to 20 minutes, and serve.

DAGING KETJAP (Fried Pork)

1 lb (½ kg) lean pork
2 tbs peanut oil
1 clove crushed garlic
1 finely chopped onion

3 oz (80 ml or 6 tbs) soya sauce
2 tbs water
1 tsp lemon juice
1 tsp brown sugar

Cut the pork into bite-sized cubes and brown in hot oil. Add garlic and onion. Fry together for 3 minutes.

Blend soya sauce with water, lemon juice and sugar and pour the mixture over the pork and simmer uncovered 12–15 minutes.

GORENG ATI (Liver)

2–3 tbs peanut oil	1 lb (500 grs or 2 cups) calf's liver,
1 finely chopped onion	cut in thin strips
1 finely chopped clove garlic	salt

Heat the oil and fry onion and garlic. As soon as these are done, move them to one side and quick-fry the liver on high heat for 2–3 minutes. Just before serving, sprinkle with salt.

SHREDDED OMELETTE, FOR RIJSTAFEL

1–2 tbs butter or oil	pinch salt and chilli powder
3–4 chopped spring onions	3–4 tbs soya sauce
1 peeled, chopped tomato	4 eggs
4 oz (125 grs or ½ cup) ham, cut	
in thin strips	

Heat the butter or oil and fry the onions until soft. Add tomato and cook together for 2–3 minutes. Add ham, season with salt, chilli and half the soya sauce. Cook for 3 minutes. Beat the eggs and stir into the pan, cover, lower heat to minimum and cook until done. Remove omelette, shred finely, sprinkle with remaining soya sauce and serve.

NASI GORENG (Indonesian Fried Rice)

This is a delicious and satisfying dish, a meal in itself, excellent for using up leftovers of cooked meat, poultry, fish, prawns, ham, vegetables, etc.

4 Servings

8 oz (250 grs or 1 generous cup) uncooked rice
2 oz (125 grs) dried shrimps
6 oz (180 ml or 12 tbs) peanut oil
2 finely chopped onions
1 finely chopped clove garlic
1 fresh shredded chilli or ½ tsp chilli powder
8 oz (250 grs or 1 cup) diced cooked meat (or chicken or fish)
3 eggs for omelette
salt and pepper
thinly sliced cucumber

Wash rice and cook in 12 oz (360 ml or 1½ cups) water for 10 minutes. Drain thoroughly, spread on a large dish and leave to cool. Soak the dried shrimps (available from Chinese food shops) in enough water to cover.

Heat oil in a large frying pan or a Chinese *wok*. Fry the onions until they turn transparent. Add garlic and chilli, fry for 3 minutes. Add meat and fry for 2 minutes, stirring all the time. Add rice.

Drain shrimps and add to rice. Fry on a fairly high flame stirring frequently, until the rice turns a pale golden colour. Season to taste. Put on a heated serving dish and keep hot.

Make Shredded Omelette (p. 74) using only the eggs seasoned with salt and pepper. Arrange omelette on top of the rice, garnish with cucumber and serve piping hot.

BURMESE COCONUT RICE

4 tbs *ghee* (see Clarified Butter)	1½ pints (¾ litre or 3 cups)
1 small chopped onion	coconut milk (p. 16)
8 oz (250 grs or 1 cup) rice	pinch salt

Heat *ghee* in a pan and fry the onion, without allowing it to brown. Add rice and fry together for 2 minutes, stirring to impregnate the rice with the onion-flavoured *ghee*. Add coconut milk, season with salt. Start cooking on a fairly brisk heat, then reduce to very low and simmer until all coconut milk is absorbed.

KEDGEREE

4 Servings

    3 oz (90 grs or 6 tbs) butter
    8 oz (250 grs or 1 cup) flaked cooked smoked haddock
    8 oz (250 grs) well drained boiled rice
    2 chopped hard-boiled eggs
    salt and pepper
    1 tbs chopped parsley
    2 raw eggs
    2 tbs single cream

Melt butter in a pan and heat the fish, stirring well. Add rice, chopped eggs and parsley. Season to taste.

Beat raw eggs with cream, stir into the pan, heat through and serve.

RICE CROQUETTES

To make rice croquettes mix cooked rice with enough white sauce (p. 16) to make a thick mixture. Season, bind with egg and leave on a shallow dish or a plate to cool. Shape into croquettes, roll in breadcrumbs, then beaten egg and once more in breadcrumbs. Leave for 20–30 minutes to set. Deep fry until golden, drain on kitchen paper and serve with tomato, mushroom or any other sauce.

Savoury rice can be mixed with chopped fried onion, or mushrooms, or any fish, meat or vegetable leftovers.

To make sweet croquettes, use dessert rice.

RICE RINGS

Savoury rice rings are made of rice pilaf or risotto (p. 83) or rice cooked in stock, well seasoned and bound with egg.

To form the rings, which serve as borders for a vast variety of dishes, press the cooked rice into a well buttered ring mould, put in the oven for a few minutes just before serving. Turn the rice out of the mould on to a heated serving dish. Fill the middle of the ring with any prepared ingredients; sliced liver or kidneys in a sauce of your choice, any mixture of vegetables, mushrooms or eggs, diced chicken or meat in sauce, etc.

Rice rings provide a good opportunity of stretching into a substantial dish and presenting the the leftovers in a decorative form.

For rice borders for sweet dishes, use dessert rice (p. 93).

RICE AND LOBSTER SOUFFLÉ

4 Servings

    8 oz (250 grs or 1 cup) rice
    2 pints (1 litre or 4 cups) concentrated fish stock (p. 9)
    4 oz (125 grs or 8 tbs) butter
    8 oz (250 grs or 1 cup) diced lobster meat
    2–3 tbs sherry
    2 tbs grated Parmesan cheese
    salt and pepper
    4 egg yolks
    4 stiffly beaten whites of egg

Cook the rice (p. 61) using fish stock instead of water for 20 minutes.

Heat 1 oz (30 grs or 2 tbs) butter lightly toss the lobster for half a minute, sprinkle with sherry and simmer for 3 minutes. Add lobster to rice, blend in cheese and remaining butter adding and stirring it in in small pieces. Allow to cool. Season to taste. Beat in the yolks, one by one. Mix well.

Fold in whites of egg, pour the rice and lobster mixture into a buttered soufflé mould and bake in a pre-heated moderate oven 375°F (Gas 4) for 15 minutes. Serve at once.

TURKISH PILAV

6 Servings

    3 oz (90 grs or 6 tbs) butter
    1 lb (½ kg or 2 cups) veal cut in cubes
    2 onions finely chopped
    2 pints (1 litre or 4 cups) stock or water with a bouillon cube
    6 stalks white celery
    1 green pepper, chopped
    8 oz (250 grs or 1 cup) Patna rice, well washed
    1 tsp garlic salt
    1 tsp cayenne pepper

Heat the butter and cook the veal and onions for 10 minutes. Add the stock and slowly bring to boil. Add celery, pepper, seasoning and rice. Cover with a napkin, then the saucepan lid and simmer for 45 minutes. Serve hot.

MUSHROOM PILAF, UZBEK STYLE

3–4 Servings

    1 pint (½ litre or 2 cups) stock
    salt
    2 oz (60 grs or 4 tbs) butter
    8 oz (250 grs or 1 cup) rice
    ¾ lb (360 grs or 4 cups) fresh button mushrooms
    1–2 tbs strong meat gravy (opt)
    1 gill (1 dcl or ½ cup) sour cream or yoghurt
    freshly grated pepper
    3–4 peeled sliced tomatoes
    parsley

Season stock, add 1 tablespoon butter and bring to the boil. Wash and drain the rice thoroughly, add to stock, stir once, cover, boil fast for 5 minutes. Lower heat and simmer gently for 12 minutes. Remove from heat. Leave to stand for half an hour. Stir gently with a wooden spoon.

Heat the remaining butter and cook the mushrooms on low heat for 8–10 minutes. Flavour with good meat gravy, stir in sour cream, heat through without boiling, check seasoning.

Arrange the rice in a ring, fill the centre of the dish with mushrooms and their sauce, surround with a border of tomato slices, decorate with parsley and serve at once.

SAN FRANCISCO BARBECUE RICE

4–6 Servings

    2 oz (60 grs or ½ cup) seeded, finely chopped green pepper
    2 oz (60 grs or ¼ cup) sliced spring onions
    3 tbs butter
    8 oz (250 grs or 1 cup) rice
    1½ tsp salt
    1 lb (½ kg or 2 cups) fresh peeled tomatoes
    ½ pint (¼ litre or 1 cup) water
    ¼ pint (1 dcl or ½ cup) dry white wine
    6 oz (180 grs or 1 cup) Cheddar cheese, cut in cubes

Fry the pepper and onions in butter gently for 3–4 minutes. Add rice and continue to fry lightly together until the rice colours a pale golden and the vegetable becomes soft. Sprinkle with salt, add tomatoes, water and wine, cover, simmer on low heat until the rice is done and the liquid absorbed (20–25 minutes). Stir in cheese, cover, remove from heat and allow the rice to stand a few minutes for cheese to soften and melt slightly. This rice can be served as a course by itself and makes an excellent accompaniment to any barbecue dish.

SOUTH CAROLINA RICE

4 Servings

 1 large pkt frozen black-eyed peas
salt and pepper
3–4 tbs butter
8 oz (250 grs or 1 cup) long grain rice
2 tsp bacon fat
2 sliced onions
½ pint (¼ litre or 1 cup) stock or water with a bouillon cube
pinch mixed herbs
3–4 tbs red wine

Bring 1 pint (½ litre or 2 cups) salted water to the boil, put in black-eyed peas, allow to come up to the boil again, season with pepper and taste for salt, adding more if necessary. Stir in 2 table-spoons butter, cover and simmer on very low heat for 30–35 minutes.

Cook the rice until tender and the water is absorbed. Stir in bacon fat.

Simmer onions in stock until they become soft and the liquid evaporates.

Mix black-eyed peas, rice, onions and the herbs. Add remaining butter and the wine, stirring very gently. Heat through and serve.

ONION RICE, SWISS STYLE

4 Servings

8 oz (250 grs or 1 cup) rice
1 lb (½ kg or 4 cups) sliced onions
2 tbs butter
2 tbs water

salt and pepper
4 oz (125 grs or 1 cup) grated Emmentaler cheese

Cook the rice until tender. Keep hot in a serving dish. Heat butter in a pan, add water and put in the onions in a thick layer. Season with salt and pepper, cover and simmer on low heat until the liquid evaporates and the onions become soft and pale golden.

Shake the pan from time to time to prevent sticking. Pile the onions in an even layer over the rice. Sprinkle the top with grated cheese, put under the grill for a few minutes to melt the cheese and serve.

PAELLA À LA VALENCIANA

For all Spanish rice dishes or *paella*, a large, deep frying-pan is essential. It is *paella*, the pan, which gave the dish its name.

Paella is the most typical of Spanish dishes and is not difficult to make. As it relies on the blending of flavours for its effect, the more varied the ingredients, the greater the success.

8–10 Servings

    3 tbs oil
    1 jointed chicken
    1 lb ($\frac{1}{2}$ kg or 2 cups) pork, cut in large dice
    1 finely chopped onion
    3 ripe tomatoes, peeled and chopped
    1$\frac{1}{2}$ lb (750 grs or 3 cups) rice
    $\frac{1}{2}$ lb (250 grs or 1 cup) runner beans
    $\frac{1}{2}$ lb (250 grs or 1 cup) peas
    1 doz artichoke hearts (opt)
    3 red peppers, seeded and sliced
    $\frac{3}{4}$ lb (360 grs or 1$\frac{1}{2}$ cups) fish (hake, eel, etc.) cut in pieces
    1 crayfish, cut in pieces
    $\frac{1}{2}$ pint (250 grs or 1$\frac{1}{2}$ cups) peeled prawns
    a few slices octopus
    1 pint ($\frac{1}{2}$ litre) mussels
    1 tsp salt
    $\frac{1}{2}$ tsp pepper
    a pinch of saffron
    2$\frac{1}{2}$ pints (1$\frac{1}{4}$ litre or 5 cups) stock

Heat the oil. Add chicken and pork. Brown lightly, add onion. When the onion is golden add tomatoes. Cook for a few minutes then put in the rice and simmer for 10 minutes. Add runner beans or peas, artichoke hearts and cook for five minutes. Add peppers and fish, crab or lobster, shrimps or prawns, octopus and any other interesting sea food. Scrub mussels, rinse well, discard all open ones. Test carefully: they should shut tightly if given a sharp tap. Add to rice. Season to taste and boil fast for 8 minutes. Reduce heat and simmer for 8 minutes. Add the saffron and stock or water with a bouillon cube. When the rice is cooked and all the water has been absorbed, put the paella in the oven for five minutes to give it a nice golden colour. Take it out of the oven and let it stand for a couple of minutes 'to settle' before serving.

REGENCY RICE

4–6 Servings

   3 oz (90 grs or 6 tbs) ham
   1–2 tbs butter or oil
   1 lb (½ kg or 2 cups) rice
   ½ lb (250 grs or 2½ cups) mushrooms
   pinch of saffron
   ½ lb (250 grs or 1 cup) chicken livers
   1 bay leaf
   salt and pepper
   1 pint (½ litre or 2 cups) white sauce (p. 16)

Chop the ham and fry it, add rice and cook seasoned with salt and pepper, saffron and bayleaf as for the Spring Rice (p. 82). Put the rice into a mould, press well and turn out on to a dish. Keep warm. Chop the mushrooms and the livers, fry and mix with the sauce. Pour the sauce, etc., over the rice and serve.

BASQUE RICE

6 Servings

   1 onion
   oil for frying
   1 lb (½ kg or 2 cups) sliced hake
   1 clove chopped garlic
   big bunch parsley

   1 lb (½ kg or 2 cups) rice
   3 pints (1½ litre or 6 cups) boiling
      water
   salt and pepper
   bay leaf

Chop and fry the onion lightly in oil for 3–4 minutes. Add garlic, parsley and rice. Add boiling water, season, put in bay leaf, simmer for half an hour and serve.

RIOJA RICE

4–6 Servings

   ½ lb (250 grs or 1 cup) ham
   3 oz (90 grs or 6 tbs) *chorizo*
   3 tbs butter
   1 small chopped onion
   1 lb (½ kg or 2 cups) rice
   1½ pints (¾ litre or 3 cups) stock
   salt and pepper
   pinch of allspice
   1 bay leaf
   2 red peppers grilled and sliced (p. 45)
   ½ pint (2 dcl or 1 cup) tomato sauce (p. 15)

Chop and fry the ham and the *chorizo* in butter, remove and in the same fat fry onion. When the onion becomes transparent, add the rice and fry it lightly. Pour in the stock, season, put in the bay leaf and the spices and cook for 18–20 minutes. When the rice is cooked, put it into a mould, turn out, garnish with fried ham, *chorizo* and grilled pepper. Pour the tomato sauce over it and serve.

RICE WITH TOMATO SAUCE AND MAYONNAISE

4 Servings

    1 onion
    3 tbs oil
    1 lb ($\frac{1}{2}$ kg or 2 cups) rice
    1$\frac{1}{2}$ pints ($\frac{3}{4}$ litre or 3 cups) water
    $\frac{1}{2}$ pint (2 dcl or 1 cup) tomato sauce (p. 15)
    $\frac{1}{2}$ pint (2 dcl or 1 cup) mayonnaise (p. 13)

Chop the onion and fry lightly, then add the rice and cook slowly for 7 to 8 minutes. Pour in the water, cook on a high flame for 8 minutes, then simmer for another 8 minutes. Put in the oven to brown lightly and serve with tomato sauce and mayonnaise.

RICE FISHERMEN STYLE

6–8 Servings

2 gills (250 ml or 1 cup) olive oil	6 oz (180 grs) conger eel
2 chopped onions	6 oz (180 grs) sea bass or halibut
1 lb ($\frac{1}{2}$ kg or 3 cups) peeled chopped tomatoes	6 oz (180 grs) prawns
	6 small crayfish
bouquet garni	1 dozen small mussels or clams
4 pints (2 litres or 8 cups) water	pinch saffron
1 tbs salt	2–3 cloves garlic
pinch freshly ground pepper	1 lb ($\frac{1}{2}$ kg or 2 cups) rice
6 oz (180 grs) monkfish	

Heat the oil and cook onions until they brown lightly. Add tomatoes, *bouquet garni*, water, salt and pepper. Bring to the boil, add all fish heads and trimmings and simmer to make a good fish stock. Cook for 18–20 minutes and strain.

Wash the fish, cut into portions. Wash the shell-fish and scrub the mussels. Toss the mussels in a little water in a frying-pan over a high flame until they open and discard half the shells. Put all fish, shell-fish and mussels (or clams) into a pan, add the prepared stock and simmer gently for 6–7 minutes. Pound the saffron with garlic in a mortar, dilute with a tablespoon stock and add to pan. Simmer for a further 6–7 minutes. Remove from heat.

Draw off 2 pints (1 litre or 4 cups) of the liquid in which the fish was cooked. Bring to the boil in another pan, sprinkle rice into it and cook on low heat for 20 minutes. Arrange the rice in a dish. Reheat the fish and serve with the rice on a separate dish.

F

WHITE RICE À LA CUBANA

4–6 Servings

1 lb ($\frac{1}{2}$ kg or 2 cups) rice	2 peeled, sliced cloves garlic
2 whole peeled cloves garlic	salt and pepper
3 tbs olive oil	

Boil rice in 5 pints (2$\frac{1}{2}$ litres or 10 cups) of water with a tablespoon salt. Sprinkle the rice in after water comes to the boil, add whole garlic cloves, stir, cover and simmer for 15 minutes. Drain, rinse with cold water, discard garlic and drain rice thoroughly again. Heat oil and fry sliced garlic until it browns, remove garlic, put rice into garlic-flavoured oil, cook, stirring for 3–4 minutes, check seasoning and serve.

RICE À LA CUBANA WITH EGGS

4–6 Servings

Prepare rice as described in White Rice à la Cubana, arrange on a serving dish and keep warm. Allowing one egg per portion, fry them in oil or butter, season with salt and pepper, arrange on rice, sprinkle with chopped parsley and serve.

As a variation, rice cooked in this manner can also be garnished with cooked sliced runner beans, tossed in oil, peeled, chopped fried tomatoes and slices of *chorizo*.*

** Chorizo* hard Spanish paprika-spiced sausage, available in good delicatessen shops.

SPRING RICE

6 Servings

cooked cauliflower	3 tbs lard
$\frac{1}{2}$ lb (250 grs or 1 cup) peas cooked with shallots (see p. 44)	1 lb ($\frac{1}{2}$ kg or 2 cups) rice
small bunch cooked asparagus tips	salt and pepper
12 cooked artichoke hearts	1 bay leaf
3 oz (90 grs or 6 tbs) diced ham	$\frac{1}{2}$ tbs butter

Cook all the vegetables, drain and save the water. Fry the ham in lard, add rice and fry until golden. Add the seasoning and 1$\frac{1}{2}$ pints ($\frac{3}{4}$ litre or 3 cups) of the water in which the vegetables were cooked for every cup of rice. When the water boils, add the vegetables and go on cooking gently until the water evaporates. Put in a hot oven with a small piece of butter on top for a few minutes before serving.

RISOTTO ALLA MILANESE (RICE MILAN STYLE)

6 Servings

    1 lb (500 grs or 2 cups) rice
    4 oz (125 grs or ½ cup) butter
    1 finely chopped onion
    2–2½ oz (60–75 grs or 4–5 tbs) diced raw beef marrow
    4 pints (2 litres or 8 cups) hot strained chicken broth
    4–5 saffron 'threads' (or small pinch saffron powder)
    salt
    4 oz (125 grs or 1 cup) grated Parmesan cheese

Heat half the butter and fry the onion lightly to soften and make it transparent. Do not allow it to brown.

Add beef marrow and cook gently together for 2–3 minutes, stirring and making sure the onion does not colour at all. Add rice, cook on low heat for a couple of minutes, stirring to coat it evenly with the onion-flavoured butter and to enrich it with marrow. Start adding broth ½ pint (2 dcl or 1 cup) at a time. Stir gently and continue to add broth as the rice absorbs it.

Soak the saffron threads in a cupful of hot broth. When the rice has been cooking for 20 minutes strain the saffron flavoured broth into it and stir well. Check seasoning and add more salt if necessary. By this time all the liquid should be absorbed and the rice should be soft but not sticky.

Add remaining butter and 2 tablespoons cheese. As soon as the butter and cheese blend in, serve the risotto with grated cheese and more butter for those who want it.

RISOTTO ALLA MILANESE WITH MARSALA

Follow instructions for Risotto Alla Milanese, but omit beef marrow and substitute 4–5 tablespoons Marsala.

RISOTTO VARIATIONS

By following the basic risotto recipe you can adapt by adding whatever principal ingredient is available or desirable: mushrooms lightly fried in garlic-flavoured butter or with a finely chopped onion, chicken livers, lobster, prawns or any shellfish, and any vegetable you like.

VENETIAN RISOTTO

Cook the rice as described in the recipe for Risotto alla Milanese, but omit saffron and beef marrow and use fish stock (p. 9) instead of chicken broth.

Just before the end of cooking, toss scampi (allowing 6–8 per portion) in hot garlic-flavoured butter, season to taste and stir the shell fish into the risotto.

Then blend in additional butter and grated cheese as described.

CHICKEN AND GAMMON RISOTTO

4 Servings

    3 oz (90 grs or 6 tbs) butter
    1 finely chopped onion
    1 crushed clove garlic
    1–2 chopped stalks celery
    1 chopped carrot
    4 oz (125 grs or 1¾ cups) sliced mushrooms
    3 peeled chopped tomatoes
    pinch chopped basil (or thyme)
    8 oz (250 grs or 1 cup) diced chicken and gammon
    1 gill (1 dcl or ½ cup) white wine
    salt and pepper
    2 pints (1 litre or 4 cups) chicken broth
    12 oz (360 grs or 1¾ cups) rice
    2–3 tbs grated Parmesan cheese

Heat half the butter and lightly fry onion, garlic, celery and carrot for 4–5 minutes. Add mushrooms, toss quickly in the pan. Add tomatoes and basil and allow to simmer for 2–3 minutes. Add chicken and gammon, moisten with wine, season to taste. Add 1 gill (1 dcl or ½ cup) broth, cover and simmer for 25–30 minutes.

Add rice and proceed to cook, adding broth a cupful at a time as described in the recipe for Risotto alla Milanese.

When all the broth has been absorbed and the rice is done, stir in the remainder of butter and the grated cheese.

RISOTTO VERDE (GREEN RICE)

Mix plain Risotto alla Marsala (p. 83), without saffron, flavouring it with 4–5 tablespoons spinach purée (p. 50).

SHERRIED RISOTTO

4–6 Servings

    1 finely chopped onion
    4 oz (125 grs or ½ cup) butter
    8 oz (250 grs or 1 cup) rice
    1 pint (½ litre or 2 cups) stock or water with a beef cube
    2 oz (60 ml or 4 tbs) sherry
    salt and pepper
    4 oz (125 grs or 1 cup) grated Parmesan cheese

Fry the onion lightly in half the butter until transparent and pale golden. Add rice and cook on low heat, stirring frequently until it turns yellow. Add stock and sherry, season to taste, bring to the boil, reduce heat, cover and simmer gently for 20–25 minutes, until all liquid is absorbed. Carefully but thoroughly stir in the remaining butter and the cheese. Serve with green salad.

SARTÙ

The fact that the Neapolitans, who know all about pasta dishes, have singled out *Sartù* to be their principal rice speciality is a recommendation in itself. The main thing against it is that it takes a long time to prepare. The best time to attempt it is when we have more giblets than the stock will take, such as Christmas.

6–8 Servings

    1–2 sets turkey or 2–3 sets of chicken giblets
    1 chopped onion
    1 small chopped carrot
    1 stalk celery
    small bay leaf
    salt and pepper
    water
    4 oz (125 grs or 1¾ cups) fresh sliced mushrooms
    8 oz (250 grs or 1 cup) minced lean beef
    1 thick slice crustless bread
    milk
    1 crushed clove garlic
    1 tbs chopped parsley
    1–2 eggs
    oil for frying
    12 oz (360 grs or 1¾ cups) rice
    butter
    4–5 tbs breadcrumbs
    8 oz (250 grs or 1 cup) cooked green peas
    2–3 sliced hard-boiled eggs (opt)
    4 oz (125 grs or ⅔ cup) diced Mozzarella (or Bel Paese) cheese
    1 pint (½ litre or 2 cups) Tomato sauce (p. 15)
    4–5 tbs grated Parmesan cheese

Cook all the giblets, except the liver, with onion, carrot, celery and bay leaf, seasoned to taste and covered with 1 pint (½ litre or 2 cups) water. Bring to the boil and then simmer on low heat for 2 hours. Add liver and mushrooms, cook for 5–6 minutes. Remove all giblets including the liver and cut into bite-size pieces. Take out mushrooms and put with giblets.

Mix minced beef with bread soaked in milk and squeezed out, garlic, parsley, seasoning and eggs. Shape into little rissoles and fry in oil, to brown on both sides. Drain.

Drop the rice into boiling salted water and allow to boil fast from 15 to 20 minutes, depending on quality. Start tasting after 14 minutes. Do not overcook, the dish will be completely ruined if you allow your rice to go mushy.

Drain, rinse with cold water, shake off surplus liquid and starch, put in a shallow uncovered dish, and place in a *warm* oven to dry off. The oven must not be hot. If you think it might be too warm, leave the oven door open. Or dry off the rice by leaving it in a shallow uncovered dish over a pan of boiling water for a few minutes.

Now, with all the ingredients ready, you can proceed to put the *Sartu* together. Butter a large ovenproof dish and sprinkle the bottom and sides with breadcrumbs. Put in half the rice and spread it over the bottom and sides of the dish, thus forming a shell. Into this rice shell put in little beef rissoles, giblets, mushrooms, peas and slices of egg. Cover with a layer of diced cheese and half the tomato sauce. Sprinkle with 1–2 tablespoons of strained giblet broth. Cover with the rest of the rice, moisten with 1–2 tablespoons giblet broth, smooth the top to enclose all the ingredients inside it. Pour remaining tomato sauce on top, sprinkle with breadcrumbs in a fairly thick layer, and finish off with a sprinkling of grated Parmesan cheese. Preheat the oven to 375°F (Gas 4). Bake the *Sartù* for half an hour.

ITALIAN RICE SOUFFLÉ (WITH CHICKEN LIVERS AND MARSALA)

6 Servings

    8 oz (250 grs or 1 cup) rice
    2 pints (1 litre or 4 cups) chicken broth or water with stock cube
    2–3 tbs grated Parmesan cheese
    4 oz (125 grs or ½ cup) butter
    2 tbs flour
    salt and pepper
    8 oz (250 grs or 1 cup) chicken livers, cut in thin strips
    2 tbs Marsala
    4 beaten yolks of egg
    4 whites of egg, beaten stiff

Cook the rice in chicken broth for 18–20 minutes. At the end of cooking stir in the cheese and half the butter. Remove from heat.

Season the flour with salt and pepper, dredge the liver with it, fry in butter to brown, then add Marsala and simmer for 5 minutes. Add to rice and mix well. Leave until lukewarm. Grease a large soufflé dish and pre-heat oven to 375°F (Gas 4). Stir yolks into the rice and chicken liver mixture, blend well, check seasoning.

Fold in whites of egg, put the mixture into the prepared soufflé dish and bake for 15–17 minutes. Serve at once.

RICE WITH FOUR CHEESES
(RISO A QUATTRO FORMAGGI)

4 Servings

    12 oz (360 grs or 1¾ cups) rice
    2 oz (60 grs or 4 tbs) each diced Bel Paese, Provolone and Gruyère cheeses
    melted butter
    2 oz (60 grs or 4 tbs) grated Parmesan cheese

Cook and drain the rice. Put in layers into a buttered ovenproof dish, alternating with layers of mixed diced cheese, sprinkling each layer with a little melted butter. Finish off with a layer of rice, sprinkle with melted butter and grated cheese, bake in the oven pre-heated to 425°F (Gas 6) long enough to heat through, melt the cheese and brown the top.

RICE WITH FISH, PUNJAB STYLE

6 Servings

    1½ lb (500–750 grs) fish fillets (hake, cod, haddock)
    1½ cups rice
    3 tbs butter
    1 tsp turmeric
    2 chopped sprigs coriander
    1 tsp garam-masala (p. 10)
    small pinch chilli powder
    1 tsp salt
    1 tbs lemon juice
    1 chopped onion
    3 pints (750 ml or 2½ cups) hot water
    ½ pint (200 grs or 1 cup) cooked, shelled prawns

Wash the fish, wipe with a cloth and cut into portions. Wash the rice and leave in water while preparing the other ingredients. Heat half the butter, add turmeric, coriander, chilli powder, garam-masala and a good pinch of salt. Cook this herb mixture for 2 minutes, moisten with lemon juice, then continue to cook over a lively flame, stirring all the time, until any surplus moisture evaporates. Add fish and fry on both sides, allowing it to pick up as much of the herb mixture as will adhere, patting lightly with a fish slice. Be careful not to break the fish portions. Cook for 5 to 6 minutes and remove from pan.

In a saucepan big enough eventually to take all the ingredients, heat the rest of the butter and fry the onion. Drain the rice, add to saucepan, season with salt, mix well, cook for 2 minutes, add the herbs and juices left from frying the fish, stir to mix well, add hot water, bring to the boil, reduce heat, cover and simmer for 30 minutes. Stir the rice mixture gently with the clean handle of a wooden spoon, put the portions of fish on top, cover and simmer for 7 to 8 minutes, garnish with prawns and serve.

BOMBAY CAULIFLOWER PULAO

Follow instructions for Rice With Peas, Indian Style and substitute a medium size cauliflower divided into flowerets for peas.

RICE WITH PEAS, INDIAN STYLE

6 Servings

    12 oz (375 grs or 1½ cups) rice
    2 tbs ghee (see clarified butter p. 9)
    4–5 cloves
    2 cinnamon sticks
    1 tsp caraway seeds
    ½ tsp turmeric
    1½ tsp salt
    12 oz (375 grs or 1¾ cups) shelled peas or (1 large pkt frozen peas)
    1 pint (600 ml or 2½ cups) hot water

Wash the rice and leave covered with cold water for 45–50 minutes. Heat the ghee with cloves, cinnamon, caraway seeds and turmeric, cook for 2–3 minutes on very low heat, stirring all the time. Drain the rice, add to fried spices, season with salt. Mix and fry together on low heat for 5 minutes, stirring. Add peas, mix gently.

Add water, increase heat, stir until it comes to the boil, cover, reduce heat to low and cook for 25–30 minutes.

KASHA (BAKED BUCKWHEAT)

1 lb (500 grs or 2⅔ cups) buck-wheat	2 oz (60 grs or 4 tbs) butter
1 tsp salt	water

Sort the buckwheat and pick out any black grains. Roast it in an ungreased frying pan, stirring and taking care not to burn, until pale golden. Put in an ovenproof dish, season with salt, stir in butter and pour in enough boiling water to cover. Bake in a slow oven 275°F (Gas 2) for 2½ to 3 hours.

RUSSIAN KASHA OR RICE AND SALMON COULIBIAC

6–8 Servings

Brioche dough (p. 17) or Puff pastry (p. 17)
Velouté sauce (p. 15)
4 oz (125 grs or ½ cup) buckwheat or rice
1 lb (½ kg or 2¾ cups) cooked, peeled, boned salmon
1 finely chopped onion
3–4 sliced hard-boiled eggs
2–3 tbs chopped parsley, chervil and tarragon
4 oz (125 grs or 8 tbs) melted butter
salt and pepper
1 egg yolk mixed with 1 tsp water

The coulibiac is better made with brioche dough, but it is also very good made of puff pastry.

Prepare dough or pastry and the sauce. Cook the kasha or rice and cool. Flake or cut salmon into very thin slices. Lightly fry the onion in a tablespoon butter. Add to it the mushrooms which were cooked in the sauce. (Or lightly fry some sliced mushrooms in butter.)

Roll out the pastry into a thin rectangle and cut in two. Place one of the sheets of rolled out pastry on a lightly buttered baking sheet, moisten the edges. Leaving the edges uncovered, spread a layer of kasha or rice on the pastry evenly. Follow with a layer of egg slices, then salmon. Season with salt and pepper. Sprinkle with chopped herbs, onions and mushrooms. Spoon some melted butter over each layer. Finish off with the remaining kasha or rice. Season, sprinkle liberally with butter. Cover with the second sheet of pastry, press down to seal the edges.

If using brioche dough, brush with yolk, prick with a fork to provide outlet for steam and bake in a hot oven 425°F (Gas 6) for 30–35 minutes.

If using Puff pastry, put in a refrigerator for half an hour. Then paint the whole surface with egg and bake in a hot oven for 20 minutes.

KASHA (BUCKWHEAT) AND MUSHROOM PIE

6–8 Servings

Quick Puff Pastry (p. 17)
1 lb (½ kg or 2⅔ cups) buckwheat
4 tbs butter
1 finely chopped onion

½ lb (250 grs or 3 cups) finely
  sliced mushroom
juice of ½ lemon
salt and pepper
beaten egg

Cook the buckwheat as described (see Kasha above).

Fry the onion in 2 tablespoons butter until soft. Add mushrooms, toss together for 3–4 minutes, add to buckwheat, sprinkle with lemon juice, season with salt and freshly grated pepper, and blend in remaining butter.

Roll out three-quarters of the pastry leaving the rest to make the top. Line a pie dish and fill it with buckwheat and mushroom mixture.

Roll out the remaining pastry, cover the pie, crimp the edges, make a slit in the centre to allow steam to escape during baking, and put the pie in a refrigerator for 25–30 minutes.

Pre-heat the oven to 425°F (Gas 6).

Brush the pie with egg, bake for 25–30 minutes.

RICE AND MUSHROOM PIE

As above, substituting rice for buckwheat.

RICE SALADS

Rice lends itself admirably to salad treatment, because it is neutral enough to combine harmoniously with other flavours and is delicious with cold sauces and dressings.

You can either use cooked rice or cook the rice specially for a salad, in which case stir some oil into it as soon as it is drained and before it gets cold. Season with salt and pepper, sprinkle with lemon juice or tarragon vinegar and mix with grated carrot and chopped spring onions, or diced celery and red or green seeded and thinly sliced peppers, peeled and quartered tomatoes, sliced hard boiled egg, stoned olives, cooked or raw mushrooms, thinly sliced and tossed in lemon juice, chopped basil or parsley, thinly sliced gherkins, diced cooked meat, ham, chicken or any other poultry or game, cheese cut in bite-size cubes, cooked peeled prawns or shrimps. A delicious combination is rice and crab or lobster meat, dressed with mayonnaise and garnished with peeled grapefruit wedges, but there is no limit to variations.

Using rice as a basic ingredient, innumerable attractive salads can be made, with the help of your imagination and whatever is available in your kitchen.

RICE AND SPINACH TIMBALE

3 Servings

    1 lb (500 grs) cooked chopped spinach (p. 50)
    4 oz (125 grs) cooked rice
    3 tbs melted butter
    3 oz (90 grs or ¾ cup) grated cheese
    salt and pepper
    ½ tsp sugar
    pinch grated nutmeg
    1 tsp lemon juice

Put the spinach in a mixing bowl.

Pour 2 tablespoons melted butter over rice and add to spinach. Add 2 oz (60 grs or ½ cup) cheese, season with salt and pepper, sprinkle with sugar, nutmeg and lemon juice and mix well.

Put the rice and spinach mixture into a well buttered ovenproof dish and sprinkle the top with the remaining melted butter. Stand the dish in a *bain-marie* (pan of boiling water) and put in the oven pre-heated to 350°F (Gas 4). Bake for 30 minutes. Run a knife around the edge of the dish and turn the timbale out on to a heated serving dish. Sprinkle with remaining grated cheese and serve.

WILD RICE

Wild rice is a great delicacy and terribly expensive. It is the native of the American continent and there was a time, unbelievable as it may seem, when it was considered as food only by the American Indians and wild mallard.

It is the Indians who introduced wild rice to white man.

Abundant crops are gathered on many of the Canadian lakes particularly Manitoba. It grows best of all in shallow lakes.

Until comparatively recently the Indians depended on wild rice as source of food for the cold winters. One of the methods of harvesting is in teams of two men to a canoe. They make their way into the rice beds, the man in front bends the plant, beats it so that the grain rains into the boat while the second man rows. This type of harvesting produces surprising results. A team of two men can gather several hundred pounds of rice in a day.

Wild rice swells to approximately four times its normal size when cooked. For best results soak wild rice in water over night.

WILD RICE WITH PRAWNS
4 Servings

   1 cup wild rice
4 cups clear chicken stock (or water with a bouillon cube)
salt
4 tbs butter
1 large chopped onion
1 clove chopped garlic
8 oz (250 grs or 3 cups) sliced mushrooms
1 seeded chopped green pepper
1 gill (1 dcl or ½ cup) dry white wine
pepper
1 tbs cornflour
12 oz (375 grs or 1½ cups) cooked peeled prawns

Wash the wild rice in several waters and leave to soak for an hour before cooking. Drain, put in a saucepan with 3 cups of chicken stock, add a pinch of salt, cover and bring to the boil. As soon as boiling is established, reduce heat, remove lid and cook for 30 minutes, without stirring. The rice should not need any draining, all the liquid ought to be absorbed. When done, add a tablespoon of butter to the rice. Keep warm. Heat 2 tablespoons of butter and lightly fry the garlic, onion, mushrooms and pepper, add wine and the rest of the stock, simmer for 5 minutes, season to taste. Blend cornflour with 2 tablespoons cold water, stir into the sauce, cook until the sauce thickens, add prawns and remove from heat.

Arrange the rice as a border in a buttered ovenproof dish, fill the centre with the prawns and their sauce, dot with small pieces of butter, put in a moderate oven 375°F (Gas 4) for 15 to 20 minutes and serve.

Rice Desserts

Rice forms the basis of many exquisite sweet dishes. Dessert rice can be made into borders, to be filled with fruit, sweet croquettes and various puddings.

DESSERT RICE

6 Servings

2 pints (1 litre or 4 cups) milk
flavouring: vanilla pod, lemon or
    orange peel, rose water, or
    orange blossom water
4 oz (125 grs or 9 tbs) rice

$2\frac{1}{2}$ oz (75 grs or 5 tbs) sugar
1 oz (30 grs or 2 tbs) butter
$\frac{1}{4}$ tsp salt
4 raw yolks

Bring the milk gently to the boil with the flavouring of your choice. Remove from heat and leave.

Wash the rice, bring to the boil in water, drain at once, rinse and drain thoroughly again.

Strain the milk, add the rice to it with the sugar, butter and salt. Stir gently, bring to the boil, then cover and simmer on lowest possible heat either on the top of the stove or, better still, in the oven, for half an hour, without disturbing the rice. Remove from heat, taste, add more sugar if necessary, carefully stir in yolks and use for hot rice desserts.

For cold rice desserts, cook as above and when done stir in 1 gill (1 dcl or $\frac{1}{2}$ cup) fresh cream.

RICE FLANS

1 flan case baked 'blind' (pie
    shell) p. 17
2–3 tbs chopped crystallised fruit

dessert rice (above)
sugar
1–2 tbs Kirsch

Fill the flan case with dessert rice mixed with crystallised fruit, sprinkled with Kirsch, or other liqueur. Do not fill right to the top, but leave an edge of $\frac{1}{8}$-inch ($3\frac{1}{2}$ mm). Sprinkle with sugar and bake in a moderate oven 375°F (Gas 4) for 25–30 minutes.

There are innumerable variations on this theme. You can fill the flan case ¾ full of dessert rice, top with halved fresh peaches or apricots dipped in Kirsch and sprinkled with sugar, or with sliced pineapple, or apples, or quartered pears, sliced bananas, dipped in rum and sprinkled with brown sugar, cooked or preserved plums, cherries, etc.

MERINGUED RICE FLAN

Prepare rice flan as described (p. 93) using dessert rice mixed with crystallised or fresh diced fruit, sprinkled with Kirsch and sugar. Cover with meringue, sprinkle with fine sugar and bake in a very hot oven to set and colour the meringue lightly.

RICE GATEAU

Cook dessert rice as described. Coat a charlotte mould with caramel, i.e. heat the mould with a few tablespoons of sugar moistened with a little water, until sugar becomes brown. Rotate the mould so that its inside becomes evenly coated with the caramelised sugar.

Fill the mould with dessert rice, put in a *bain-marie* (a shallow pan of hot water) and bake in a moderate oven for 25–30 minutes.

This Rice Gateau can be served either hot or cold.

RICE À L'IMPÉRATRICE

4 oz (125 grs or ½ cup) vanilla-flavoured dessert rice
3 tbs chopped crystallised fruit
1–2 tbs Kirsch or other liqueur
½ pint (2 dcl or 1 cup) custard
gooseberry jelly
2 gills (2 dcl or 1 cup) whipped cream

Cook the rice as described and allow to cool.

Soak the fruit in Kirsch and mix with rice. Stir in custard. Spread gooseberry jelly in a ½-inch (1¼ cm) layer on the bottom of a charlotte mould. Fold whipped cream into rice, spoon the mixture into the mould and chill.

Turn out on to a chilled dish before serving.

RICE FRITTERS

Using cooled dessert rice, make sweet fritters by dropping a tablespoon of the rice mixture into hot oil and deep frying until golden on both sides. Drain well. Sprinkle with sugar and serve.

For savoury fritters, use pilaf, risotto, or any savoury rice, mixed with finely chopped fried onion, parsley or other herbs, minced or finely chopped cooked meat, chicken or ham, liver, fish or prawns.

Or flavour the savoury rice fritters with grated cheese, chopped mushrooms, tomatoes, etc.

BAKED RICE PUDDING

    3 oz (90 grs or 6 tbs) rice, washed and drained
    1 oz (30 grs or 2 tbs) butter
    3 oz (90 grs or 6 tbs) sugar
    2 pints (1 litre or 4 cups) creamy milk
    nutmeg

Butter a pie dish, put in rice, butter, sugar and milk. Sprinkle with grated nutmeg and put in the lower part of a slow oven (300°F, Gas 2) for 30 minutes. Stir and continue to bake for another 15–20 minutes. Stir again and then leave undisturbed for 2 hours.

The above is the classical English recipe for rice pudding, but it can be varied in many ways. You can flavour it with lemon rind instead of nutmeg, slip a fresh bay leaf into it, add raisins and almonds to it, beat in an egg or two, enrich it with cream, colour it with grated chocolate or strawberry jam. You can pour caramelised sugar on it and glaze the top or cover it with meringue and bake it in the oven, as described in the recipe for Meringued Rice Flan.

ORIENTAL RICE CAKE

    4 oz (125 grs or 1 cup) self-raising flour
    pinch baking powder
    3 oz (90 grs or 6 tbs) butter
    2 oz (60 grs or 6 tbs) sultanas
    1 oz (30 grs or 2 tbs) currants
    2 oz (60 grs or 6 tbs) seedless raisins
    1 tbs grated lemon rind
    4 oz (125 grs or 1 cup) ground rice
    small pinch salt
    2 well whisked eggs
    1 gill (1 dcl or $\frac{1}{2}$ cup) milk
    3 oz (90 grs or 6 tbs) soft brown sugar

Sift flour with baking powder into a bowl. Cut butter into small pieces and rub it into the flour. Add sultanas, currants, raisins, lemond rind and rice. Season with a little salt. Stir well. Beat the eggs into the milk, then stir the mixture into the rice and flour. Add sugar, mix thoroughly, put into a lightly greased tin and bake in a very moderate oven 350°F (Gas 3) for $1\frac{1}{4}$ hours. Test for readiness: insert a knife in the centre of the cake – if it comes out dry, the cake is baked. If not, continue for another 15–20 minutes, testing again after 10 minutes.

Pasta Dishes

PASTA

This glory of Italian cuisine covers an endless variety of products of all shapes and sizes, from minute *acini di pepe*, so called because they look like pepper corns, to large ribbed *rigatoni* cut into 3-inch ($7\frac{1}{2}$ cm) lengths, from little stuffed *cappelletti*, shell like *conchiglie*, *lasagne*, *tagliatelle* and tube-like *ziti* $\frac{1}{2}$-inch ($1\frac{1}{4}$ cm) in diameter.

Good pasta is made of wheat flour. Some products are made of a mixture of water and flour, others are made with eggs.

The first requisite for cooking pasta is a really large deep saucepan. Allow a gallon (4 litres or 4 quarts) of boiling water and 2 tablespoons salt per pound of pasta.

Bring water to the boil and feed the pasta into it a little at a time, to ensure that it does not go off the boil. If the water falls below boiling point by the addition of too much pasta, it may stick together in lumps.

Long kinds of pasta, such as spaghetti or vermicelli should not be broken.

Allow to boil vigorously stirring with a long wooden spoon from time to time, to prevent sticking.

The worst thing you can do to pasta is overcook it. Pasta should be served when it still offers a pleasant resistance to the teeth – or, as the Italians say, *al dente*.

Bought varieties of pasta usually have instructions for cooking on the packet, specifying cooking time, and with some brands it is safest to stick to the instructions. There are commercial brands on the market which require only 2–3 minutes' cooking. Cooking times vary according to the thickness of pasta. The following is an approximate table of cooking times for various kinds of pasta:

Spaghetti	8–12 minutes
Spaghettini and vermicelli	6–10 minutes
Long macaroni	10–15 minutes
Shells, wheels, etc.	7–12 minutes
Tagliatelle	5– 6 minutes
Lasagne	6–10 minutes
Rigatoni	10–15 minutes

The above table of cooking times applies only to mass produced pasta products. Home made pasta will need only half the time, sometimes less.

To avoid overcooking, even with shop bought pasta, start testing after 4 minutes, and repeat every other minute. The best test is to bite a strand of pasta.

As soon as the pasta is ready to your liking, drain at once. Do not rinse with cold water – you will never get it hot again. To arrest cooking, you can pour a cup of cold water into the saucepan, stir and drain at once.

Put on a heated dish, add the sauce of your choice, kept ready and warm before you cook the pasta, and hand grated Parmesan separately. Serve immediately – pasta, like omelette, must not be kept waiting.

Quantities of pasta per serving are given in the recipes, but these can be varied to suit individual capacity and depending on whether you intend to serve pasta as a main, or an only course, or as an accompaniment or a curtain raiser. Generally speaking allow 3–4 oz (90–125 grs) of pasta to be served as *pasta asciuta* (dry pasta), as opposed to *pasta in brodo* (pasta in broth).

In China noodles and pasta dishes are almost as important in the diet of the people as rice. The variety of pasta products, the Chinese ravioli and cannelloni, is endless.

Noodles are eaten as a main course. People will often have a bowl of noodle soup or a dish of braised noodles for lunch or supper – and delicious they are, too. Noodles also play a traditional part on special occasions, particularly at birthday dinners, because they are a symbol of long life. When serving noodles, never cut them, for that 'shortens the life'.

In Japan, too, noodles and pasta play an important part, second only to rice. Among the popular varieties of Japanese pasta products there is *udon*, which looks like macaroni, *soba*, thin noodles made of buckwheat flour, and *somen*, a thin wheat vermicelli. These three kinds of noodles can be bought dry or pre-cooked, to be reheated at home. In addition there are *harusame*, a type of noodles made of soya bean powder; *shirataki*, vermicelli made of a tuberous root with a gelatinous texture; and *chasoba*, a green-coloured vermicelli made of buckwheat and green tea. Pride of place undoubtedly belongs to *soba*, which forms the basis of many noodle dishes such as *Yubasoba*, served with bean curd; *Gomokusoba*, a five-colour dish garnished with fish, prawns, eggs and vegetables; *Okame Soba* with fish and mushrooms, and many others. A dish of noodles is a must at a Japanese New Year's Eve meal, to ensure good luck throughout the year, and many people still observe the custom of presenting *soba* to their friends as a token of goodwill.

Many of the commercial brands are excellent but they cannot compare with the home made pasta. We therefore start with recipe for Home Made Bologna Noodles – *Tagliatelle*.

HOME MADE BOLOGNA NOODLES (TAGLIATELLE)

4–6 Servings

1 lb (480 grs or 4½ cups) flour
3 eggs
1 tsp salt

2–3 tbs warm water
Sauce Bolognese (p. 11)
grated Parmesan cheese

Sift the flour on to a pastry board, make a well in the middle, put in it eggs, salt and half the water. Stir the eggs with a fork, folding the flour over them until half the flour is amalgamated. Knead by hand, adding a little water at a time to prevent the paste from becoming too stiff. Equally, take care not to overmoisten. Knead for 8–10 minutes until the paste is smooth and can be formed into a ball. If it sticks to your hands during kneading, dip your hands in flour. Cut dough into 3 pieces and roll each into a paper thin sheet on a well floured board.

For rolling out large sheets of dough, a long rolling pin is useful. After rolling out, lay or hang the sheet over the back of a chair on a floured cloth and leave to dry for 30–40 minutes.

Fold the sheets into Swiss rolls and with a sharp knife cut across into strips about ½-inch (1¼ cm) wide. Shake gently with fingers to unfold the noodles, spread them on a floured cloth on the table, cover with a clean towel and leave until ready to cook. Use within one hour or store in a dry place.

Cook as described for 4 minutes, but start testing after the third minute.

Drain, mix with the sauce and serve immediately with Parmesan cheese.

GREEN TAGLIATELLE

6 Servings

1 lb (480 grs or 4½ cups) sifted flour
3 eggs at room temperature
½ lb (250 grs or 1 cup) cooked spinach purée
　　See recipe for Spinach Soufflé (p. 54)
Bolognese sauce (p. 11)
4 oz (125 grs or 1 cup) grated Parmesan cheese

Sift the flour on to a pastry board, make a well in the middle, put in eggs, spinach and salt. Mix the dough and knead as described in recipe for Home Made Tagliatelle (p. 98). Roll into a ball, leave to rest for 10–15 minutes, then divide into 3–4 portions, roll out paper thin, fold into a Swiss roll, and with a sharp knife cut crosswise into strips ½-inch (1¼ cm) wide.

Cook as described in salted boiling water for 2–3 minutes, stirring frequently. Drain, mix with sauce and serve. Hand grated cheese separately to be sprinkled on the noodles at the table.

TAGLIATELLE ALLA CREMA

4–6 Servings

1 lb (500 grs) cooked *tagliatelle* (noodles)
2 oz (60 grs or ½ cup) grated Parmesan cheese
2 tbs flour
pinch salt
pinch nutmeg
4 oz (125 grs or 8 tbs) butter
½ pint (2 dcl or 1 cup) milk
2 eggs
1 gill (1 dcl or ½ cup) single cream

Put half the cheese and the flour into a saucepan. Season with salt and add a grating of nutmeg. Gradually dilute with milk, simmer on very low heat, stirring constantly until the mixture thickens. Blend in half the butter, adding it in small pieces. Remove from heat, add the remaining cheese and butter in small pieces, stir and allow the mixture to cool a little.

Separate the eggs and one by one stir the yolks into the mixture. Whisk the egg whites until stiff.

Stir the cream into the sauce and fold the whites into it. Mix the hot, well drained *tagliatelle* with the sauce, put in a lightly buttered ovenproof dish, place in a medium oven, preheated to 375°F (Gas 4), bake for 15 minutes and serve.

TAGLIATELLE SOUFFLÉ

4–5 Servings

1 lb (½ kg) home made noodles (p. 98)
salt and pepper

Mornay sauce (p. 13)
pinch nutmeg
4 eggs

Prepare Mornay sauce as described, using Parmesan cheese. Season well and add a grating of nutmeg. Remove from heat. Cook the home made noodles as described for 4–5 minutes (shop bought noodles usually require longer cooking) and drain.

Separate the yolks from the whites and blend into the sauce, adding one yolk at a time. Make sure the sauce is not too warm, to prevent curdling.

Beat the egg whites with a small pinch of salt until very stiff and fold into the sauce.

Mix noodles with the sauce, put in a buttered soufflé mould, bake in a pre-heated oven 375°F (Gas 4) for 20 minutes and serve.

TAGLIARINI WITH CHICKEN LIVERS

4 Servings

12 oz (375 grs or 1½ cups) chopped chicken livers
2 oz (60 ml or 4 tbs) olive oil
1–1½ chopped cloves garlic
½ lb (250 grs or 1 cup) peeled ripe tomatoes
4 oz (125 grs or 1 cup) cooked green peas
salt and pepper
12 oz (375 grs) *tagliarini* (thin, narrow noodles)
grated cheese

Fry the livers in oil to brown on all sides. Add garlic and tomatoes. Cover and simmer on low heat for 20 minutes. Add peas, season to taste.

Cook the pasta in the usual way, drain, put on a heated serving dish. Pile the livers, peas and the sauce on top and serve with grated cheese.

FETTUCCINE NEAPOLITAN STYLE

Cook the ribbon noodles as described. If you are using home made pasta, start cooking the sauce at the same time. It should be fresh and takes five minutes to prepare.

2 Servings

8 oz (250 grs) fettuccine
4 tbs olive oil
3–4 sliced cloves garlic
1 lb (500 grs or 2 cups) ripe peeled tomatoes
1 tsp fresh basil (or mint) leaves
salt and freshly grated black pepper
grated Parmesan cheese

Boil the pasta.
Heat oil and lightly fry the garlic for 1 minute.

Cut the tomatoes into quarters, if they are small, halve each quarter again, if they are large. Add to garlic.

Cook for 3–4 minutes, stirring from time to time.

Tear the basil leaves into pieces, add to sauce, season.

Serve the sauce on top of well drained fettuccine. Hand grated cheese separately.

FETTUCCINE AL BURRO (EGG NOODLES WITH WHIPPED BUTTER)

6 Servings

6 oz (180 grs or ¾ cup) unsalted butter
Home made *fettuccine* (wide noodles) (p. 98)
freshly ground black pepper
8 oz (250 grs or 2 cups) grated Parmesan cheese

Whip the butter.

Cook the noodles as described, for 4–5 minutes. Drain well. Put on a heated serving dish, dress with butter, season with pepper, sprinkle with cheese and serve at once.

LASAGNE VERDI AL FORNO

Spinach-tinted green pasta
Bolognese sauce (p. 11)

Béchamel sauce (p. 11)
butter
3–4 tbs grated Parmesan cheese

Prepare the pasta as described in the recipe for Green Tagliatelle (pp. 98–99). Instead of cutting into strips, cut into oblong pieces about 3 inches (7½ cm) long and 2 inches (5 cm) wide. Observe all the rules given for home made pasta. Do not cook until the sauces are ready. Preheat the oven, set at 375°F (Gas 4). Cook the lasagne in plenty of fast boiling salted water for 5 minutes and drain. Butter a large ovenproof dish. Put into it a layer of Bolognese sauce, then a layer of Béchamel sauce, followed by a layer of lasagne.

Continue in this manner, filling the dish with layers of Bolognese sauce, Béchamel sauce and pasta. Finish with a layer of Bolognese sauce and Béchamel sauce. Sprinkle the top with an even layer of grated cheese. Scatter tiny pieces of butter over the whole surface. Bake for 20–25 minutes.

The melted cheese should form a crust on top, but the lasagne should be soft, not crisp.

In some parts of Italy, thin slices of Mozzarella or Bel Paese cheese are used instead of Béchamel sauce. But for real Bolognese lasagne, a good creamy Béchamel sauce flavoured with a grating of nutmeg, in addition to Bolognese sauce, is essential.

SPAGHETTI WITH TUNNY SAUCE

4–6 Servings

2 oz (60 grs or 4 tbs) butter
2 oz (60 ml or 4 tbs) oil
1 clove garlic
small tin tomato paste
½ pint (¼ litre or 1 cup) water

6 oz (180 grs or ¾ cup) tin tunny in oil
3 finely chopped anchovy fillets
2 tbs chopped parsley
salt and pepper
1 lb (½ kg) spaghetti

Heat butter and oil together, fry the garlic until golden and discard garlic.

Dilute tomato paste with water, add to butter and oil. Simmer for half an hour.

Flake the tunny and add, with its oil and anchovies. Stir, add parsley, season to taste and simmer for 10 minutes.

Boil spaghetti as described (pp. 96–97) for 10 minutes, stirring from time to time. Drain, mix with the sauce and serve

SPAGHETTI ALLE VONGOLE

4–6 Servings

1 lb (500 grs) spaghetti
clam sauce (p. 12)

Boil the spaghetti, to serve *al dente* (p. 96).

Drain, arrange in a heated serving dish. Pour very hot clam sauce over it and serve.

SPAGHETTI WITH ANCHOVY SAUCE

3–4 Servings

4 oz (120 ml or ½ cup) olive oil
2 cloves garlic
2–3 ripe tomatoes, peeled and chopped

4–5 finely chopped anchovy fillets
salt and pepper
12 oz (375 grs) thin spaghetti

Heat the oil, fry the garlic in it until it browns. Remove and throw away the garlic, add tomatoes, cook on low heat stirring for 15 minutes.

Add anchovies, simmer for a couple of minutes. Season to taste and bear in mind the salt content of the anchovies. Leave on lowest possible heat.

Cook spaghetti as described. Drain, mix with the sauce and serve at once.

SPAGHETTI WITH OIL AND GARLIC

4 Servings

1 lb (500 grs) spaghetti	black pepper
8 tbs good quality olive oil	1 tbs chopped basil
3–4 crushed cloves garlic	grated Parmeson cheese (opt)

Boil the spaghetti in salted water as described (pp. 96–97). While it is cooking, heat the oil with garlic, turn off heat, add basil and leave to stand until the spaghetti is ready. Drain the spaghetti, check seasoning, grate black pepper over it, mix. Pour the garlic flavoured oil over the spaghetti and serve. If you dislike eating pieces of garlic, strain the garlic flavoured oil over the pasta, and keep the basil for sprinkling over it.

SPAGHETTI OR TAGLIATELLE WITH PESTO

Pesto is a Ligurian speciality. The Genoese serve it with pasta, minestrone or as a flavouring to vegetable dishes. Sealed in a jar with a well fitting lid *pesto* can be kept for a week or so.

4 Servings

4 tbs fresh basil (or parsley) leaves
1–2 cloves garlic
2–3 tbs shelled pine nuts (or blanched almonds)
pinch salt
4 oz (120 grs or 1 cup) grated Sardo (or Parmesan) cheese
4 tbs olive oil
1 lb ($\frac{1}{2}$ kg) pasta

Pound basil in a mortar with garlic, pine nuts and a pinch of salt. Add cheese and continue to pound until the mixture is reduced to a paste. Incorporate the oil little by little, as for mayonnaise, until all has been absorbed.

Cook the pasta in the usual manner, drain, put on a heated serving dish or on individual plates, add a generous helping of *pesto* and serve.

Note: The alternatives suggested in brackets, i.e. parsley instead of pine nuts and Parmesan instead of Sardo cheese, will make a very pleasant imitation of *pesto* but to enjoy the real thing all substitutes should be avoided.

SPAGHETTI ALLA CARBONARA

4–5 Servings

  1 lb (500 grs) spaghetti
  2 tbs oil or butter
  4–5 bacon rashers or slices of ham
  2 oz (60 ml or 4 tbs) dry white wine
  2–3 beaten eggs
  2 oz (60 grs or ½ cup) grated Parmesan cheese
  salt and black pepper

Cook the spaghetti in the usual way. While the spaghetti is cooking, start preparing the carbonara garnish. Heat oil or butter and fry the bacon until crisp. Moisten with wine and simmer gently until the liquid evaporates.

Drain the spaghetti, put on a heated serving dish and keep hot. Add half the cheese to the eggs and stir the mixture into the pan with the bacon. Season with salt and freshly ground black pepper. Cook as you would scrambled eggs, but only until the eggs just begin to set. Pour the bacon and egg mixture on the pasta, mix and serve with the remainder of the grated cheese.

SPAGHETTI ABRUZZO STYLE

4 Servings

  2 tbs pork dripping
  ½ clove chopped garlic
  1 chopped onion
  3 oz (90 grs or 6 tbs) shredded pickled pork
  1 lb (500 grs or 2 cups) ripe peeled, chopped tomatoes
  salt and freshly grated black pepper
  1 lb (500 grs) spaghetti
  4 oz (125 grs or 1 cup) grated Pecorino (or Parmesan) cheese

Heat pork fat in a saucepan, add garlic and onion and fry lightly for 2–3 minutes. Add pork and cook, stirring, for 10 minutes. Add tomatoes and season the sauce. Leave to simmer low.

Boil spaghetti, drain well, mix with hot sauce and serve with grated cheese.

SPAGHETTI UMBRIAN STYLE

4 Servings

  2 oz (60 ml or 4 tbs) olive oil
  1 clove garlic
  4–5 pounded anchovy fillets
  1 small tin tomato paste
  3 gills (3 dcl or 1½ cups) warm water
  salt and pepper
  2 black or white truffles (fresh or tinned)

Heat the oil and brown the garlic to flavour the oil. Discard the garlic. Blend in anchovy paste. Dilute tomato paste with water and stir into the pan. Simmer on low heat for half an hour.

Cook the spaghetti. While it is boiling, chop the truffle. As soon as the spaghetti is cooked, drain well, mix with sauce, sprinkle with truffles and serve.

SPAGHETTI WITH PARSLEY OIL SAUCE

4 Servings

1 lb (500 grs) spaghetti
8 tbs olive oil
3–4 chopped cloves garlic

5–6 tbs finely chopped parsley
generous grating of black pepper
grated Parmesan cheese

Cook spaghetti as described.

While the spaghetti is cooking, heat oil with garlic, cook on low heat for 5–6 minutes, until pale golden. Add parsley, cook on low heat for 2–3 minutes.

Drain spaghetti, put in a heated serving dish. Pour sauce over it, season with freshly grated black pepper, sprinkle with cheese, mix and serve at once.

MACARONI ALLA PIZZAIOLA

4 Servings

2 oz (60 ml or 4 tbs) olive oil
1 clove garlic
1½ lb (¾ kg or 3 cups) ripe tomatoes (egg shaped, if possible) or tinned
   Italian tomatoes
salt and pepper
pinch basil or *origano*
1 lb (½ kg) macaroni
2 oz (60 grs or ½ cup) grated Parmesan cheese

Start by making the Pizzaiola sauce. Heat oil and fry the garlic until golden, after which discard it. Peel and chop tomatoes and add to the oil. Season with salt and pepper, add basil or *origano*, stir and leave to simmer for 20–25 minutes.

When the sauce is half done, i.e. after it has been simmering for 10–12 minutes, put salted water to boil for the macaroni. Cook macaroni as described, stirring frequently to prevent sticking. Drain, mix with sauce and cheese on a heated serving dish and serve at once.

MACARONI, NEAPOLITAN STYLE

4 Servings

1 lb (500 grs) macaroni
Pizzaiola sauce (p. 14)

3 oz (90 grs or ¾ cup) grated Parmesan cheese

Cook macaroni in salted boiling water, stirring from time to time, until done. They should be tender yet firm. Drain. Serve with Pizzaiola sauce and cheese.

MACARONI CALIFORNIAN STYLE

5–6 Servings

1 lb (500 grs) uncooked macaroni
2 tbs slightly softened butter
8 oz (250 grs or 1½ cups) cubed cheddar cheese
pinch salt
pinch dry mustard
2 beaten eggs
8 oz (240 ml or 1 cup) milk
1 gill (1 dcl or ½ cup) single cream
1 gill (1 dcl or ½ cup) dry white wine
3 tbs chopped green peppers
2 oz (60 grs or ½ cup) grated breadcrumbs
2 tbs melted butter

Combine all ingredients, except breadcrumbs and melted butter. Mix well, put in a buttered ovenproof dish. Mix breadcrumbs with melted butter and sprinkle on top of macaroni.

Cover and bake in a pre-heated moderate oven 350°F (Gas 3) for 45–50 minutes. Remove cover, turn off heat, leave the dish to stand for 10 minutes and serve.

RAVIOLI

Ravioli is one of the varieties of pasta envelopes filled with various ingredients. They are delicious served either as *pasta asciutia* or in a clear broth and are not really difficult to make. Ravioli can be made of ordinary noodle paste but proper ravioli paste should contain a little butter.

RAVIOLI PASTE

12 oz (375 grs or 3 cups) flour
pinch salt
2 eggs
1 oz (30 grs or 2 tbs) softened butter
scant ½ pint (240 ml or 1 cup) warm water

Sift flour and salt on to a pastry board, make a well in the middle, break the eggs into it, fold the flour into them as for noodle paste. Add butter, knead and little by little incorporate enough water to make a smooth stiff dough. Cover with a floured cloth and leave to stand for 10 minutes. Divide into two or three parts, depending on the size of your pastry board, roll out on a floured board until very thin.

Spread the rolled out paper-thin sheets of paste on a cloth and cover with another cloth, to prevent drying and preserve elasticity.

For filling, put a teaspoon of stuffing on one sheet of paste, allowing about $1\frac{1}{2}$ inches ($3\frac{3}{4}$ cm) intervals between the little mounds of filling. Trace demarcation lines between the spoonfuls of filling with a pastry brush dipped in beaten egg. Cover with a second sheet of paste, then proceed to cut out your ravioli.

The cutting can be done either by running a pastry wheel along the traced out lines, which will give you little square pillow shapes, or by pressing out with a round pastry cutter, not more than $1\frac{1}{2}$ inches ($3\frac{3}{4}$ cm) in diameter. Keep the cut out ravioli on a lightly floured board; do not overlap or stack them in layers. Cover with a floured cloth until ready to use. Ravioli can be made in advance and kept in a refrigerator between sheets of waxed paper.

Boil them as you would any pasta, in plenty of salted boiling water. Cook home made ravioli for 4 minutes. Carefully remove from pan with a perforated spoon, transfer to a heated serving dish and serve with melted butter, or Tomato sauce (p. 15) and grated Parmesan cheese.

SPINACH AND CHICKEN FILLING FOR RAVIOLI

8 oz (250 grs or 1 cup) cooked spinach purée (p. 50)
8 oz (250 grs or 1 cup) cooked finely chopped or minced chicken
2 oz (60 grs or $\frac{1}{2}$ cup) grated breadcrumbs
2 oz (60 grs or $\frac{1}{2}$ cup) grated Parmesan cheese
$\frac{1}{2}$ clove pounded garlic (opt)
1 tbs finely chopped parsley
salt
freshly ground black pepper
2 beaten eggs

Combine all the ingredients, bind with eggs, mix well, check seasoning and use the filling as described.

VEAL FILLING FOR RAVIOLI

8 oz (250 grs or 1 cup) diced lean veal
2 oz (60 grs or 4 tbs) butter
stock or water with stock cube
1 gill (1 dcl or $\frac{1}{2}$ cup) red wine

1 slice crustless bread
milk
4 oz (125 grs or ½ cup) cooked drained spinach
2 oz (60 grs or ½ cup) grated Parmesan cheese
2 tbs finely chopped onion
salt
freshly grated black pepper
2 beaten eggs

Fry the veal in butter to brown on all sides, add enough stock just to cover the bottom of the pan and simmer for 15 minutes. Moisten with wine and cook until tender.

Pour enough milk over the bread to soak it, then squeeze out surplus milk.

Pass the veal, bread and spinach through a mincer. Add cheese, and onion, season with salt and pepper to taste, blend in eggs to bind and mix thoroughly.

SPINACH FILLING FOR RAVIOLI

8 oz (250 grs or 1 cup) cooked spinach
2 tbs butter
salt and pepper
2 oz (60 grs or ½ cup) grated Parmesan cheese
pinch nutmeg
1 beaten egg

Drain the spinach well and while still hot, chop and stir butter into it. Season, add cheese, a grating of nutmeg and the egg to bind the mixture. Mix well.

CREAM CHEESE FILLING FOR RAVIOLI

12 oz (360 grs or 1½ cups) cream cheese
1 oz (30 grs or 2 tbs) butter
3 oz (90 grs or ¾ cup) grated Parmesan cheese
1 egg
½ tbs chopped parsley
pinch salt
freshly grated black pepper
pinch nutmeg

Blend all ingredients together into a smooth mixture and drop spoonfuls on rolled out ravioli paste as described.

CAPPELLETTI

6 Servings

Pasta dough (see recipe for home made Bologna noodles (p. 98)
1 chicken breast

2 tbs butter
1 lb (500 grs or 2 cups) cottage cheese
1 egg
1 egg yolk
salt and pepper
¼ tsp nutmeg
tomato sauce (p. 15)
4 tbs grated Parmesan cheese

Fry the chicken in butter to brown evenly on both sides and chop or mince finely. Put in a mixing bowl, add cottage cheese, egg, yolk, season with salt and pepper to taste, sprinkle with nutmeg and mix well.

Roll out the dough into paper-thin sheets on lightly floured board. With a pastry cutter, cut into little circles. Put a teaspoon of stuffing in the middle of each circle, fold over one side and shape into 'little hats'. Press to seal the edges firmly. Boil the cappelletti in 1 gallon (4 litres or 4 quarts) of fast-boiling salted water for 5 minutes or until tender. Drain, put on a heated serving dish and serve with tomato sauce and grated cheese.

Cappelletti are also delicious cooked in chicken broth and served as a soup.

CANNELLONI

6 Servings

Prepare home made pasta by following the recipes given for *tagliatelle* or *ravioli* (pp. 98 and 106). Knead until smooth, roll out paper-thin and cut the rolled out sheets into 3-inch (7½ cm) squares.

Boil a few at a time (5–6) in plenty of salted boiling water for 4–5 minutes.

Take out of the water with a slotted spoon and straighten out each square on a damp kitchen towel, taking care not to tear. When all squares are cooked, allow to cool and fill with the fillings suggested for *ravioli* or *cappelletti* (pp. 106, 108). Do not overstuff. Put 1–1½ tablespoons of the stuffing on half of each square, leaving the edge free. Starting at the filled end, roll up tightly, arrange in a buttered ovenproof dish, laying them side by side, sprinkle with melted butter, grated Parmesan cheese and 1 gill (1 dcl or ½ cup) of clear chicken or veal stock and bake uncovered in a moderate oven (375°F, Gas 4) for 15 minutes.

Cannelloni can be prepared in advance. After filling, keep between sheets of waxed paper in a refrigerator. See instructions for Ravioli.

CHICKEN AND MUSHROOM FILLING FOR CANNELLONI

2 tbs butter
8 oz (250 grs or 3½ cups) finely sliced fresh muchrooms
1 lb (250 grs or 2 cups) chopped cooked chicken
salt and white pepper
½ pint (2 dcl or 1 cup) creamy white sauce (p. 16)
1 egg yolk

Lightly fry the mushrooms in butter. Mix with chicken. Season to taste with salt and pepper.

Blend yolk into the sauce, enriched with a few tablespoons cream.

Combine mushroom and chicken mixture with the sauce, fill and finish off cannelloni as described.

CHEESE AND SAUSAGE FILLING FOR CANNELONI

8 oz (250 grs) fresh pork sausages
12 oz (360 grs of 1½ cups) cream cheese
4–5 tbs grated Parmesan cheese
salt and pepper
1–2 beaten eggs *or* 1 gill (1 dcl or ½ cup) Tomato sauce (p. 15)

Prick the sausages with a fork, put in a shallow frying pan with enough water to cover and cook until the water evaporates, about 25–30 minutes. Brown the sausages on all sides in the fat yielded by them. Allow to cool, skin and mash with a fork. Mix sausage meat with cheese, blend into a smooth mixture, season to taste, add egg or Tomato sauce to bind and fill the *cannelloni* as described.

FILLING FOR LENTEN CANNELLONI

12 oz (360 grs or 1½ cups) cream cheese
8 oz (250 grs or 2 cups) grated Parmesan cheese
2 oz (60 ml or 4 tbs) thick white sauce or cream
small pinch grated nutmeg
salt and pepper
1 beaten egg

Combine all ingredients in the order listed, mix well and use to fill the *cannelloni* as described.

CHICKEN AND CHICKEN LIVER FILLING FOR CANNELLONI

In addition to the stuffings suggested above, *cannelloni* are delicious filled with a mixture of chicken breast and livers, fried lightly in a little butter, minced together with a few slices of smoked ham, mixed with grated Parmesan, seasoned with salt and white pepper and bound with fresh butter and cream.

STUFFED RIGATONI

4 Servings

    Tomato sauce (p. 15)
1 lb (500 grs) rigatoni
1 tbs finely chopped onion
1 chopped clove garlic
2 tbs oil
12 oz (360 grs or 1½ cups) good minced beef
2 oz (60 grs) mozzarella or provolone cheese, better still both
3 oz (90 grs) mortadella
salt and freshly ground black pepper
grated cheese

Have the sauce ready.

Cook the rigatoni, as described. Drain and allow to cool. Prepare filling: fry onion and garlic in oil for 2 minutes. Add mince and brown lightly. Chop the mozzarella, provolone and mortadella together and add to beef. Remove from heat, season to taste, mix well, and allow the stuffing to cool.

Fill the rigatoni either by piping the stuffing into them with a forcing bag, or splitting each one in half lengthwise, stuffing and reshaping the pasta.

Arrange the filled rigatoni in layers in an oiled ovenproof dish, spoon a little sauce and sprinkle some grated cheese on each layer. Bake in a moderate oven 375°F (Gas 4) for 20 to 25 minutes. Serve piping hot in the same dish.

FARFALLE (PASTA BOWS OR BUTTERFLIES) WITH MUSHROOMS, BACON AND PEAS

4 Servings

    2 tbs butter
1 chopped onion
3 thick bacon rashers, cut in small dice
12 oz (360 grs or 1½ cups) shelled peas
2–3 tbs water
8 oz (250 grs or 3½ cups) fresh sliced mushrooms
salt and pepper
1 lb (500 grs) pasta bows
3 tbs grated Parmesan cheese

Heat butter and cook the onion until it softens. Add bacon, peas and water. Cook for 10–12 minutes. Add mushrooms and continue to cook gently, stirring from time to time. Season to taste.

Have the salted water on the boil. As soon as the mushrooms are added to the bacon and peas, begin to cook the farfalle. Taste for readiness, drain.

Mix the farfalle with the mushrooms, bacon and peas, sprinkle with grated cheese and serve.

CALIFORNIAN PASTA SALAD

4 Servings

    12 oz (360 grs or 3 cups) macaroni or pasta shells
    salted water
    12 oz (360 grs or 1½ cups) ham, cut in large dice
    2 sliced hard boiled eggs
    3 tbs chopped celery
    1–2 onions, cut in very thin rings
    2 tsp capers
    mayonnaise (p. 13)
    paprika
    parsley, divided into small sprigs

Boil the pasta as described, or follow instructions on the packet. Do not overcook – whichever variety you choose must be *al dente*. Drain, rinse with cold water and drain thoroughly again. Allow to cool.

Combine with ham, eggs, celery, onion rings, capers and mayonnaise. Mix carefully, sprinkle with paprika and garnish with tiny bouquets of parsley.

GNOCCHI

4 Servings

    ¾ pint (360 ml or 1¾ cups) milk
    4½ oz (135 grs or 12 tbs) farina
    3 tbs butter
    1 beaten egg
    1 oz (30 grs or 4 tbs) grated Parmesan cheese
    1 tsp salt
    Mornay sauce (p. 13) or Mushroom sauce (p. 13) or Tomato sauce (p. 15)

Heat milk in a double boiler, stir into it farina, 2 tablespoons butter and salt and cook for 20 minutes. Add egg and cheese, whisk to blend. Pour in a ½-inch (¾ cm) layer into a greased pan and chill. Cut into small squares, diamonds or any other shape and lay in a buttered ovenproof dish. Cover with Mornay, Mushroom or Tomato sauce, put in a very moderate oven 350°F (Gas 3) and bake for half an hour.

TETRAZZINI RAMEKINS

6 Servings

3 tbs butter
4 oz (125 grs or 1¾ cups) sliced
  mushrooms
8 oz (250 grs or 1 cup) diced
  chicken

salt and pepper
4 tbs dry white wine
Mornay sauce (p. 13)
1 lb (500 grs) spaghetti
grated Parmesan cheese

Heat 2 tablespoons butter and lightly fry mushrooms and chicken, stirring from time to time. Season to taste, sprinkle with wine and cook, stirring, until the wine evaporates.

Cook the spaghetti in salted water for 10 minutes and drain. Add to them the mushrooms and chicken mixture and the sauce. Mix well.

Divide the mixture in six individual baking dishes, buttered and sprinkled with grated cheese. Sprinkle the top with grated cheese and dot with the remaining butter in small pieces. Preheat the oven to 375°F (Gas 5) and bake for 20 minutes.

RUSSIAN PEL'MENI

Egg noodle paste (p. 98)
½ lb (250 grs or 1 cup) each
  minced beef and minced lean
  pork

1 finely chopped onion
salt and pepper
2–3 tbs cold water

Prepare noodle paste, roll out thin and cut out small circles. Mix beef, pork and onion, season with plenty of salt and pepper, add a little cold water and knead to blend well. Put a teaspoon of the meat stuffing on each circle of rolled out pastry.

Don't put in too much filling, to allow for the accumulation of delicious juices between the dough and the meat. And don't make pel'meni too big – they look much nicer if they are bite-size.

Dip your fingers in flour to give you more gripping power and seal the edges, forming a plump-centred semi-circle, then join the tip together. Pel'meni should look like generously proportioned *cappelletti* (p. 108).

Leave on a floured board or a sheet of waxed paper in a refrigerator until ready for use.

Siberians, who know all about *pel'meni* and consume vast amounts of them, consider this preliminary chilling essential. Among Siberian housewives it is a recognised custom to keep several hundred *pel'meni* in their cold cellar, or just outside the window in a bag, if it is freezing outside. They are then ready to be dropped into boiling broth or salted water, as required.

H

PEL'MENI IN BROTH

Boil the *pel'meni* in broth, dropping them a few at a time so that the broth does not go off the boil. After 4 minutes or as soon as they float up to the surface, start testing. If you like your broth very clear, cook the *pel'meni* in salted boiling water and serve in piping hot broth, sprinkled with chopped dill or parsley.

SIBERIAN PEL'MENI

Prepare *pel'meni* as described. Boil in salted boiling water until done. Remove with a perforated spoon, arrange in a heated serving dish, pour melted butter over them, sprinkle with chopped parsley and serve.

Serve vinegar and mustard dressing separately.

To make vinegar and mustard dressing, mix a teaspoon of made mustard with 3 tablespoons vinegar, blend well.

PEL'MENI WITH SOUR CREAM

Cook *pel'meni* as described in recipe for Siberian *pel'meni* using only beef filling. Serve with sour cream poured over them instead of melted butter.

FRIED PEL'MENI

Boil *pel'meni* with beef filling in salted water for 3 minutes. Remove with a perforated spoon, shaking off all water. Fry in sizzling butter to brown very lightly on both sides and serve. Serve sour cream and chopped dill or parsley separately.

HOME MADE NOODLES, CHINESE

4 Servings

1 lb ($\frac{1}{2}$ kg or 4 cups) flour   2 eggs
$\frac{1}{2}$ tsp salt

Using 12 oz (375 grs or 3 cups) flour, salt and eggs, make a dough. Knead well and roll out thinly. (To ensure evenness of rolling out, always roll forward.) Use the rest of the flour for sprinkling the pastry board to prevent sticking. Fold the dough and cut into strips – fine ones for soup, wider ones for braising, frying, etc. Sprinkle a little flour over the strips and loosen them out on a board into long strips. (If not using immediately, cover with a damp cloth.)

Allow 3 pints (1$\frac{1}{2}$ litres or 6 cups) water to boil 1 lb ($\frac{1}{2}$ kg) noodles, and always put the noodles into boiling water, separating them with a pair of chopsticks to prevent sticking.

Boil for 5 minutes and drain.

CRISPY NOODLES WITH CHICKEN AND BAMBOO SHOOTS

4 Servings

1 lb (½ kg) home made Chinese noodles (p. 114)
1 lb (½ kg or 2 cups) lard or oil for deep frying
1–2 tbs peanut oil
4 oz (125 grs or ½ cup) diced chicken meat
salt and pepper
2 oz (60 grs or ⅓ cup) sliced bamboo shoots
3 oz (60 grs or 1 cup) bean sprouts
2 oz (60 grs or ¾ cup) sliced mushrooms
1 medium sized chopped onion
1 tsp cornflour
2 tbs cold water
1 dessertspoon soya sauce
few drops sesame oil

Boil the noodles for 5 minutes, rinse under running cold water and drain well.

Heat the fat. Arrange the noodles in a strainer or frying basket and deep fry for 5 minutes, by which time they should be crispy and golden. Press the noodles to sides of frying basket to form a 'nest'.

Take the basket out of the fat, shake to allow surplus fat to drip off, transfer noodle nest to a heated serving dish and keep hot. Cook chicken in peanut oil for 1 minute. Season with salt and pepper to taste.

Add bamboo shoots, bean sprouts, mushroom and onion. Cook together for 1 minute, stirring all the time.

Dilute cornflour with water and soya sauce, blend into the pan and cook for 1 minute.

Sprinkle with sesame oil and serve the whole on top of the noodles.

VELVET NOODLES

6 Servings

3 oz (90 grs or 6 tbs) lean pork, cut in thin small slices
1 oz (30 grs or ½ cup) fresh sliced mushrooms
2 tsp light soya sauce
1 tsp cornflour
1 pint (½ litre or 2 cups) stock or water with a bouillon cube
1 Cos lettuce, shredded
1 tsp Ve-Tsin
salt
6 oz (180 grs) rice noodles
2 pints (1 litre or 2 cups) salted boiling water

H*

Sprinkle pork and mushrooms with 1 teaspoon soya sauce and the cornflour. Mix well.

Put in a pan, add stock, bring to the boil and simmer for 8 minutes. Add lettuce, remaining soya sauce and Ve-Tsin. Stir gently and cook for 30 seconds.

Taste for seasoning and, if necessary, add salt.

Bring noodles to the boil in salted water, simmer for 30 seconds and drain.

Arrange noodles on a heated serving dish, pour sauce over them, heaping pork, mushrooms and lettuce on top and serve.

RICE NOODLES HONG KONG STYLE

2 Servings

    6 oz (180 grs or 2 cups) thick rice noodles
    ½ lb (250 grs or 1 cup) lobster meat, diced
    3 oz (90 grs or 1 cup) bean sprouts
    1 oz (30 grs or 4 tbs) sliced mushrooms
    2 oz (60 grs or ¼ cup) sliced cucumber
    2 oz (60 grs or ¼ cup) sliced water chestnuts
    2 oz (60 grs or ¼ cup) sliced bamboo shoots
    1 oz (30 grs or 2 tbs) sliced celery
    1 oz (30 grs or 4 tbs) sliced onion
    1 tbs oil
    ½ tsp salt
    1 tsp sugar
    1 dessertspoon soya sauce
    stock

Put the noodles in a bowl, cover with hot water and leave to stand for 30 minutes. Heat oil in pan and sauté the lobster for 1 minute. Add all the vegetables and cook together for 1 minute. Add salt, sugar, soya sauce and enough stock to cover. Cook for 1 minute, add drained noodles, cook for 2 minutes and serve.

CHINESE NOODLE OR WUN TUN PASTE

This dough is used for Chinese noodles, wun tun and various other patties and dumplings.

4–6 Servings

    1 lb (480 grs or 4 cups) flour   water
    2 eggs

Mix flour and eggs and add enough water to make pliable dough. Roll out paper thin.

Then, if used for Chinese noodles, fold over 6–8 times, dusting the layers with plain flour, and cut into strips ⅛-inch wide. If using for wun tun or patties, cut into 2-inch squares.

ANKE'S CHAR SHIU BAO
(Chinese roast pork dumplings)

6 Servings

4 tbs lean roast pork, finely chopped
4 tbs peanut oil
1 tsp soya sauce
pinch salt
pinch Ve-Tsin

1 tbs sugar
1 tsp cornflour
2 tsp oyster sauce
6 oz (180 grs or 1½ cups) flour
½ tsp baking powder

Fry the pork in 1 tablespoon oil, stirring all the time for 45–50 seconds and sprinkle with soya sauce, salt, Ve-Tsin and 1 teaspoon sugar. Dilute half the cornflour with 3 tablespoons of cold water and stir it into the pork. Cook for 1½ minutes, stirring the mixture, which should be quite dry. Remove from heat and leave to cool. Mix remaining cornflour with oyster sauce and blend into the pork. While the pork stuffing is cooling, prepare the dough for the char shiu bao.

Sift the flour on to a pastry board, make a well in the centre, sprinkle in baking powder and remaining sugar. Add 3 tablespoons oil and 2 tablespoons cold water. Mix well and knead into a stiff dough. Cut the dough and roll into fat sausages between the palms of your hands. Break off uniform pieces, roll to the size of a ping-pong ball and flatten each into a circle about 2½ inches (6¼ cm) in diameter.

Put a portion of roast pork filling in the centre of each circle of dough and pinch up the edges with fingers, turning to shape the dumpling. Alternately, put the flattened circle of dough on a lightly floured cloth, fill with stuffing, then hold the cloth with the circle of dough in the left hand and twist the end of the cloth tightly, to mould the dough into a round bun with a twisted top.

Place each dumpling on a small square of wax paper and put them in a steamer, about 1 inch (2½ cm) apart. Steam over rapidly boiling water for 20 minutes. Serve piping hot.

HAR GOW (Chinese steamed Prawn Dumplings)

6–8 Servings

1 tbs lard
4 oz (125 grs or ½ cup) raw pork, minced
2 tbs mushrooms, finely chopped
2 spring onions, finely chopped
4 Pacific prawns, peeled and chopped
2 tbs bamboo shoots, diced
1 thin slice ginger, finely chopped
½ tsp sesame oil

pinch salt
pinch Ve-Tsin
2 tsp light soya sauce
¼ tsp sugar
1 tbs wine (or sherry)
½ tsp cornflour
2 tbs cold water
6 oz (180 grs or 1½ cups) Chinese wheat starch (or flour)
6 oz (180 ml or ¾ cup) boiling water

Heat lard in frying pan and toss the pork for 30 seconds. Add mushrooms, spring onions, prawns, bamboo shoots, ginger and sesame oil. 'Scramble' for 30 seconds, season with salt, Ve-Tsin, soya sauce and sugar. Sprinkle in wine.

Dilute cornflour in cold water, pour over the contents of the frying pan, stir well and turn out the dumpling filling into a bowl.

Mix wheat starch with hot water into a stiff dough, adding the water very gradually. Knead well, sprinkle with dry flour and roll into a long sausage. Pinch off small pieces of dough of uniform size, roll out into circles 3 inches in diameter, taking care to fray the edges by scraping them with the lip of a bowl or saucer. Put a good teaspoon of the filling in the middle of each circlet of dough, pinch the edges together to form a semi-circle, steam for 12 minutes and serve piping hot.

WUN TUN (CHINESE RAVIOLI) SOUP
6 Servings

Wun Tun paste (p. 116)
1½ lb (750 grs) pork
salt
1 oz (30 grs) dried mushrooms
6 oz (180 grs or ¾ cup) prawns, shelled
½ tsp Ve-Tsin
4 oz (125 grs or ¾ cup) spring onions, chopped

1 dessertspoon cornflour
1 dessertspoon soya sauce
1 dessertspoon brandy
1 tsp oil
1 egg
1 egg, beaten
water
2½ pints (1¼ litre 5 or cups) hot pork (or chicken) broth

Have the Wun Tun paste ready.

Mince the pork and season with salt to taste. Scald and shred the mushrooms.

Cut the dough into 2-inch (5 cm) squares. Combine pork, mushrooms, prawns, Ve-Tsin and three-quarters of the spring onions, cornflour, soya sauce, brandy, oil and 1 egg. Blend well. Place a teaspoon of this mixture on the dough. Fold over, seal with egg and round off the edge of the Wun Tun.

Boil fast for 7 minutes in plenty of water, keeping the pan uncovered. Drain and serve in bowls of hot, strained broth allowing 4–5 Wun Tun per bowl. Sprinkle with the remaining spring onions.

SHAO MAI (Pork and prawn steamed dumplings)

6–8 Servings

    Chinese noodle paste (p. 116) using half the quantity
    8 oz (250 grs or 1 cup) half-lean, half-fat pork, minced
    4 oz (125 grs or ½ cup) cooked, peeled, prawns
    1 tbs water chestnuts, chopped
    1 tbs bamboo shoots, chopped
    pinch salt
    pinch sugar
    pinch Ve-Tsin
    1 tsp light soya sauce
    pinch grated ginger
    1 tbs Chinese wine (or sherry)

Prepare the dough, knead well, wrap in a damp cloth and leave until the filling is ready.

Put pork in a mixing bowl. Reserve 6–8 prawns for decoration and chop the rest. Combine pork and chopped prawns with the rest of the ingredients, blend well.

Break off uniform pieces of dough, roll each piece into a thin circle and fray the edges by scraping with the lip of a bowl or saucer. Put 3 teaspoons filling in the centre of each piece of pastry and pinch the edges to close around the filling, but leave the top free.

Garnish the top of each *shao mai* with a whole prawn, stand in a steam cage and steam for 15 minutes. Serve at once.

BAHMI GORENG (Indonesian Fried Noodles)

6 Servings

    8 oz (125 grs) Chinese egg noodles
    4 oz (120 ml or ½ cup) peanut oil
    12 oz (360 grs or 1½ cups) finely shredded pork
    2 cloves crushed garlic
    1 large sliced onion
    2 tsp finely grated green ginger (or 3 tsp powdered ginger)
    2–3 celery stalks, chopped
    1 lb (250 grs or 1½ cups) shredded cabbage
    4 oz (125 grs or ½ cup) peas or beans
    3 oz (90 grs or 1 cup) bean sprouts
    8 oz (250 grs or 1 cup) cooked peeled prawns
    8–10 chopped spring onions
    1 tbs soya sauce
    salt and freshly ground black pepper
    Shredded omelette (p. 74)

Cook the noodles in plenty of boiling salted water for 5–6 minutes, drain and spread out on a board and leave to cool and dry out.

Heat 1–2 tablespoons oil and brown the pork lightly for 5

minutes. Remove from pan. Keep warm. Add another tablespoon oil and fry garlic, onion and ginger for 3 minutes. Remove and keep warm.

Add 2 tablespoons oil and lightly fry all the vegetables for 2–3 minutes. Remove and keep warm.

In the same pan quickly toss the prawns for 1 minute. Add pork, and all the other fried ingredients. Sprinkle with soya sauce and spring onions, season to taste with salt and pepper, stir to mix well and cook together for 2 minutes.

Heat the remaining oil in another pan and fry the noodles until pale golden. Transfer to a heated serving dish. Pile the mixture of fried pork, vegetables and prawns on top. Garnish with Shredded omelette and serve with boiled rice and Indonesian pickles (see Atjar p. 67).

NOODLES BOHEMIAN STYLE

4 Servings

1 lb (500 grs) home made noodels (p. 114)	4 tbs butter
boiling salted water	4 tbs breadcrumbs
	1–2 tbs poppy seeds

Cook the noodles in plenty of salted boiling water and drain well. Melt butter, add breadcrumbs and brown lightly. Add poppy seeds, mix well, sprinkle the mixture over noodles and serve at once piping hot.

NOODLE TIMBALE

4–6 Servings

1 pint ($\frac{1}{2}$ litre or 2 cups) Tomato sauce (p 15)
1 lb (500 grs) fettuccine noodles
2 oz (60 grs or 8 tbs) grated Pecorino (or Parmesan) cheese
2 oz (60 grs or $\frac{1}{2}$ cup) diced Bel Paese (or similar soft cheese)
2–3 cooked, sliced sausages
salt and pepper
1 tbs butter
2 tbs breadcrumbs

Have the Tomato sauce ready.

Boil the noodles as described (pp. 96–97). Drain well and mix with grated and diced cheese and sliced sausage. Season to taste and add all but 1 gill (1 dcl or $\frac{1}{2}$ cup) Tomato sauce. Mix thoroughly. Butter a baking dish, sprinkle with breadcrumbs and transfer the timbale mixture into it. Spoon the reserved sauce over the top and bake in the oven pre-heated to 375°F (Gas 4) for 20 minutes.

FULL MOON NOODLES

This is a traditional and attractive Japanese way of presenting cold noodles, very refreshing served as a summer meal.

6 Servings

    12 oz (360 grs) noodles
    1½ quarts (1½ litres) water
    salt
    18 trefoil (or long watercress stems)
    1½ pints (¾ litre or 3 cups) dashi (p. 9)
    4½ tbs shoyu
    2 tbs sugar
    pinch Aji-no-Moto
    6 raw egg yolks
    ice cubes

Cook noodles in slightly salted water, drain, rinse with cold water, drain again and leave until quite cold – better still, chill in a refrigerator. Tie trefoil in bundles of three and trim stems. Dip into boiling water for a moment, rinse with cold water and drain. Mix dashi with shoyu and sugar, add Aji-no-Moto, bring to the boil, stir, remove from heat and chill. Put noodles in deep bowls, place an egg yolk in the centre, taking great care not to break it and ruin your 'moon'. Garnish with trefoil, arranging it in a decorative loop. Add a cube of ice. Pour chilled soup over it and serve.

SAVOURY NOODLE PANCAKES

4 Servings

    8 oz (250 grs or 1 cup) very fine   salt and pepper
       noodles   butter
    2 eggs

Boil the noodles in salted water until tender, drain well. Beat the eggs lightly, add noodles, season with salt and pepper and mix.

Butter a griddle or a thick pan and taking a tablespoon of the noodle pancake mixture at a time cook them over moderate heat, to brown on both sides. Serve at once.

MANDELN (JEWISH COOKERY)

    2 beaten eggs   2 tbs oil
    6 oz (180 grs or 1½ cups) flour   1 tsp salt

Combine all ingredients to make a soft dough. Chill for half an hour. Cut off small portions at a time, dip your hands in flour and roll the dough between your hands into pencil thin sausages, then cut into $\frac{1}{2}$-inch ($1\frac{1}{4}$ cm) pieces. Bake these in a greased baking tin and bake until uniformly golden. The oven should be heated to 375°F (Gas 4). The baking process takes about 18–20 minutes. Shake the baking tin from time to time to ensure even browning. Serve in plain clear consommé.

Pasta Desserts

DALMATIAN NOODLE PUDDING

4-6 Servings

    6 oz (180 grs or 2 cups) fine noodles
    boiling salted water
    1 jar raspberry jam
    2 oz (60 grs or ⅔ cup) chopped walnuts
    3 tbs breadcrumbs
    2–3 tbs butter

Cook noodles in plenty of lightly salted boiling water and drain. Put in a layer of noodles in a well buttered ovenproof dish, cover with a generous layer of raspberry jam and sprinkle with walnuts. Continue in this way, filling the dish with layers of noodles, jam and walnuts. Sprinkle with breadcrumbs, dot with little pieces of butter and bake in a very moderate oven 350°F (Gas 3) for 30 minutes. Serve piping hot.

UKRAINIAN VARENIKI

6–8 Servings

Egg noodle paste (p. 101) 1 tbs sugar
1 lb (½ kg or 2 cups) cream cheese ½ tsp salt
2 eggs 4 tbs sour cream

Mix the cream cheese with the eggs, sugar, salt and sour cream. Roll out the pastry as for Pel'meni (p. 113), fill each circle with a teaspoon of cream cheese, and seal up the edges forming little semicircles. See that the pastry on the edges is quite thin, otherwise the double thickness may take longer to cook through. Put a few at a time into salted boiling water allowing one teaspoon salt to 1½ pints (¾ litre or 3 cups) water, and boil for 10 minutes.

Remove with a perforated spoon, serve at once piping hot, with melted butter or sour cream and sugar.

VARENIKI WITH CHERRIES

6–8 Servings

    2 lb (1 kg) cherries   Egg noodle paste (p. 101)
    6 oz (180 grs or ¾ cup) sugar   sour cream

Stone the cherries, preserving all the juice, add sugar and leave for 3 to 4 hours. Crush five or six cherry stones into fine powder, add to the cherries, cover with ½ pint (2 dcl or 1 cup) water, bring to the boil, simmer for 1 or 2 minutes and strain, keeping all the juice. Roll out the dough as described and fill each little circle with two or three cherries. Cook, remove with a perforated spoon, put in a heated serving dish and keep warm.

Boil down the strained juice left over from the cherries and allow to cool. Serve this syrupy sauce and sour cream with the vareniki.

VARENIKI WITH PRUNES

6–8 Servings

    1¼ lb (600 grs or 3 cups) prunes   Egg noodle paste (p. 101)
    2 oz (60 grs or 4 tbs) sugar   castor sugar

Boil the prunes in a little water, rub through a sieve, add sugar, simmer together to thicken the mixture and allow to cool. Roll out the paste, fill with prune *purée* and cook as described. Sprinkle with castor sugar and serve with sour cream.

POPPY SEED NOODLES

4 Servings

    Home made egg noodles (p. 101)
    3 oz (90 grs or 6 tbs) softened butter
    2 oz (60 grs or ⅔ cup) ground poppy seeds
    8 oz (240 grs or 1 cup) sugar
    grated rind of 1 lemon

Boil the noodles in lightly salted boiling water, as described, drain well. Add butter and mix well to prevent the noodles sticking. Keep hot.

Mix sugar, poppy seed and lemon rind. Sprinkle over noodles. Shake to mix and serve at once.

Glossary

AJI-NO-MOTO. Japanese seasoning powder, known as *Ve-Tsin* in Chinese cookery, excellent for bringing out flavours, based on monosodium glutamate.

BAIN-MARIE. Vessel containing hot water in which foods can be poached and various dishes and sauces can be kept hot without coming into contact with direct sources of heat.

BLIND (BAKED). Method of baking a flan, or pie shell, or any other pastry case 'blind', i.e. empty.

BOUILLON. Stock.

BOUQUET-GARNI. A faggot or bunch of herbs, normally containing three sprigs of parsley, one sprig of thyme and small bay leaf. To facilitate extraction from soups, sauces, stews, etc., tie together in a piece of muslin.

BUCKWHEAT. *Blé noir*, a variety of Saracen corn.

COULIBAC. A Russian pie, usually hot and often made of brioche dough with a filling of salmon, etc.

COURT-BOUILLON. Aromatized liquid for cooking meat, fish, vegetables. See recipes.

DASHI. Japanese stock, based on dried bonito shavings and *konbu* seawood.

FUMET. Liquid to give flavour and body to stocks and sauces, made by boiling down almost to nothing food-stuffs of various kinds, either in stock or wine.

GARAM-MASALA. Essential ingredient in most curry dishes.

GHEE. Clarified butter used in Indian cookery.

OYSTER SAUCE, as its name indicates, is made from oysters. It has the ability to blend with and intensify the flavour of a dish.

ROUX. A mixture of butter (or other fats) and flour, cooked for varying periods of time, used for thickening sauces and soups.

SAKE. Japanese rice wine used for drinking and flavouring.

SHOYU. Japanese soya sauce.

SOBA. Japanese buckwheat noodles.

SOMEN. Japanese vermicelli made of wheat flour.

SOYA SAUCE. Liquid made from soya beans – universal imparter of flavour and texture for which there is no substitute.

SUSHI. Japanese rice sandwiches.

TAMARIND. The juice of tamarind is used to impart an acid flavour in the way in which vinegar or lemon juice is used for European cooking. The tamarind fruit is steeped in water then all the fibres are removed, the juice is strained.

TEMPURA. A great Japanese speciality consisting of ingredients dipped in batter and deep fried.

TENDON. Tempura style shellfish, usually served on rice.

TURMERIC. Turmeric is widely used for various dishes on account of its aromatic qualities. It is also used for colouring rice.

VE-TSIN. See Aji-no-moto.

Index

Abon, 65
Agnolotti, *see* Ravioli, 106
Anchovy Sauce, *see* Spaghetti with Anchovy Sauce, 102
Anke's Char Shiu Bao (Chinese Roast Pork Dumplings), 117
Artichoke Hearts with Eggs and Cream, 20–21
Artichoke Hearts with Spinach, 20
Artichokes, 20
Artichokes, Braised (Jerusalem), 38
Artichokes (Jerusalem), with Rice, 38
Asparagus, 21
Asparagus à La Flamande, 21
Asparagus and Cheese Casserole, 21
Asparagus Quiche, 22
Asparagus with Caper Sauce, 21–2
Atjar (vegetable pickle for Rijstafel), 67–8
Aubergine Caviar, 22
Aubergine Moussaka, 40
Aubergines, Fried with Yoghurt (Parsee recipe), 23–4
Aubergines Sandwiched with Tomato, 23
Aubergines with Almond Sauce, Catalan Style, 23
Avgolemono Sauce (Egg and Lemon), Greek, 10
Avgolemono Soup, 59

Baby Lima Beans, 25
Baby Lima Beans with Bacon, 25
Baby Marrows (Zucchini), 40
Baby Onions in Sherry and Cream, 44
Bacchanalian Sprouts, 52
Bahmi Goreng, 119
Baked Mushrooms, 41
Baked Potatoes, 47
Baked Rice Pudding, 95
Bananas, crispy, 67

Basque Rice, 80
Batter, Tempura, 10
Bean Sambal, 66
Beans, à la Française, 27
Beans, Baby Lima, 25
Beans, Baby Lima with Bacon, 25
Beans, Broad à l'ancienne, 26
Beans, Dried white, 25
Beans, French, Burgundy Style, 26
Beans, French with Bacon crumble, 27
Beans, Red à la Bourguignonne, 25–6
Beans, String, Armenian style, 27
Beans, white with Butter, 25
Béchamel Sauce, 11
Beef, Java Style, 73
Beef Satay, 69
Beetroot Burgundy Style, 28
Beetroot in Cream, 27
Beetroot with Onions, 27
Boiled Cauliflower, 33–4
Bolognese Sauce, 11
Bombay Cauliflower Pulao, 88
Braised Celery, 36
Braised Chicory, 36
Braised Jerusalem Artichokes, 38
Braised Leeks, 39
Broad Beans à l'Ancienne, 26
Brussel Sprouts, Bacchanalian, 52
Buckwheat, Baked (Kasha), 88
Buckwheat and Mushroom Pie, 89
Burmese Coconut Rice, 75
Butter Clarified, 9
Butter, noisette, *see* chicory with noisette butter, 36

Cabbage, Red Flemish Style, 29–30
Cabbage Leaves, Stuffed Russian Style, 30
Cabbage Stuffed with Olives and Rice, 29

Cabbage with Chestnuts, Hungarian Style, 28–9
Cake, Oriental, rice, 95
Californian Pasta Salad, 112
Cannelloni, 109
Cannelloni, Lenten Filling, 110
Cannelloni Filling, Cheese and Sausage, 110
Cannelloni Filling, Chicken and Chicken Liver, 110
Cannelloni Filling, Chicken and Mushroom, 110
Cantonese Rice and Steamed Chicken, 62
Cappelletti, 108–9
Carrot Soufflé Pie, 33
Carrots à la Vichy, 32
Carrots, Andalusian Style, 32
Carrots, Californian Style, 33
Carrots Marsala, 31
Carrots, Young with Cream, 32
Carrots with Caraway Seeds, Austrian Style, 32
Casserole, Asparagus and Cheese, 21
Casserole, Spinach and Mushroom, 51
Cauliflower à la Polonaise, 34
Cauliflower, Boiled, 33–4
Cauliflower, Bombay Pulao, 88
Cauliflower in Sauterne with Almonds, 35
Cauliflower Loaf, 35
Cauliflower Pie, 34
Cauliflower, Spanish, 34
Celery, Braised, 36
Celery, Californian Style, 36
Char Shiu Bao, Chinese pork dumplings, 117
Cheese and Sausage Filling for Cannelloni, 110
Chicken and Chicken Liver Filling for Cannelloni, 110
Chicken and Gammon Risotto, 84
Chicken and Lime, 72
Chicken and Mushroom Filling for Cannelloni, 110
Chicken, Coconut, 73
Chicken Liver Sambal, 66
Chicken Satay with Peanut Butter Sauce, 69
Chicory à la Béchamel, 36
Chicory au Gratin, 36
Chicory, Braised, 36
Chicory with Noisette Butter, 36
Chinese Boiled Rice (I), 61

Chinese Boiled Rice (II), 61
Chinese Boiled Rice (III), 61
Chinese Homemade Noodles, 114
Chinese Lettuce (I), 39
Chinese Lettuce (II), 39
Chinese Mushrooms, Bamboo Shoots and Water Chestnuts, 41
Chinese Mushrooms Stuffed with Shrimps, 42
Chinese Noodle or Wun Tun Paste, 116
Chinese Rice with Mushrooms, 62
Chinese Steamed Prawn Dumplings, 117
Clam Sauce, for Spaghetti alle Vongole, 12
Clarified Butter, 9
Coconut Chicken, 73
Coconut Milk, 16
Coconut Rice, Burmese, 75
Concentrated Fish Stock, 9
Consommé, Rice, 59
Coulibiac, Kasha (or rice) and Salmon, 89
Cream Cheese Filling for Ravioli, 108
Cream of Rice Soup, 59
Cream Sauce, 12
Crispy Bananas, 67
Crispy Noodles with Chicken and Bamboo Shoots, 115
Croquettes, Potato, 47
Croquettes, Rice, 75
Cucumbers à la Crème, 37
Cucumbers Mornay, 37

Daging Ketjap, 73
Dalmatian Noodle Pudding, 123
Dashi, 9
Dessert Rice, 93
Dolmathes, Stuffed Vine Leaves, 53
Dough, Quick Brioche, for Coulibiac, 17
Dried White Beans, 25
Duchess Potatoes, 46–7
Dumplings, roast port, Chinese, 117
Dumplings, steamed, pork and prawn, Chinese, 119
Dumplings, steamed prawn, Chinese, 117

Egg Noodles with Whipped Butter (Fettucine al Burro), 101
Eggs, spiced, 70
Eggs, Duck, preserved, 70
Endive (U.S. Chicory) Loaf, 37

Farfalle, Pasta Bows or Butterflies, with Mushrooms, Bacon and Peas, 111
Fettucine al Burro (Egg Noodles with Whipped Butter), 101
Fettuccine, Neapolitan Style, 100
Fish Fillets, Spiced, 70
Fish Sambal, 65
Fish Stock, Concentrated, 9
Flan Cases, Baked Blind, 17
Flan, Onion, Swiss, 44
Flans, Rice, 93
Flans, Rice Meringued, 94
Fondue, Tomato, 52
French Beans à la Française, 27
French Beans, Burgundy Style, 26
French Beans with Bacon Crumble, 27
Fried Aubergines with Yoghurt, 23–4
Fried Pel'Meni, 114
Fried Pork, Indonesian, for Rijstafel, 73
Fried Rice, Hong Kong Style, 62
Fritters, Rice, 94
Full Moon Noodles, 121

Garam-Masala, 10
Gateau, rice, 94
Glazed Turnips, 53
Gnocchi, 112
Goreng Ati (Liver), 74
Green Risotto, 84
Green Tagliatelle, 98
Grilled Peppers, 45

Har Gow, Chinese Steamed Prawn Dumplings, 117
Hollandaise Sauce, 12
Home Made Bologna Noodles (Tagliatelle), 98
Home Made Noodles, Chinese, 114
Hong Kong Spinach, 50

Imam Bayildi, 24
Indonesian Chicken and Vermicelli, 72
Indonesian Fried Noodles, 119
Italian Rice and Cabbage Soup, 60
Italian Rice Soufflé, with Chicken Livers and Marsala, 86

Japanese Chestnut Rice, 64
Java Style Beef, 73
Jerusalem Artichokes, braised, 38
Jerusalem Artichokes, with Rice, 38
Jim Riley's Saratoga Creamed Potatoes, 46

Kasha (Baked Buckwheat), 88
Kasha and Mushroom Pie, 89
Kedgeree, 75
Kemangi, 69

Lamb Vindaloo, 68
Lasagne Verdi al Forno, 101
Leeks à la Vinaigrette, 38–9
Leeks, braised, 39
Lenten Cannelloni filling, 110
Lettuce, Chinese (I), 39
Lettuce, Chinese (II), 39
Loaf, Cauliflower, 35
Loaf, endive, 37

Macaroni alla Pizzaiola, 105
Macaroni Californian Style, 106
Macaroni Neapolitan Style, 106
Mandeln, Jewish cookery, 121–2
Marrow Moussaka, 41
Marrows, 40
Marsala Carrots, 31
Matchstick Potatoes, 45
Mayonnaise, 13
Meringue Rice Flan, 94
Mornay, cucumbers, 37
Mornay Sauce, 13
Most Precious Rice, 63
Moussaka, 40
Moussaka, Marrow, 41
Mousseline Sauce, 13
Mushroom Pie Lucerne, 43
Mushroom Pilaf, Uzbek Style, 77
Mushroom Sauce, 13
Mushrooms, baked, 41
Mushrooms, Chinese, with bamboo shoots and water chestnuts, 41
Mushrooms, Chinese stuffed with Shrimps, 42
Mushrooms stuffed with Ham, Parma Style, 42

Nasi Goreng, 74
Noisette Butter, see chicory with noisette butter, 36
Noodle or Wun Tun Paste, Chinese, 116
Noodle Pancakes, Savoury, 121
Noodle Pudding, Dalmatian, 123
Noodle Timbale, 120
Noodles Bohemian Style, 120
Noodles, Bologna (Tagliatelle) Home made, 98
Noodles, Crispy with Chicken and Bamboo Shoots, 115

Noodles, Full Moon, 121
Noodles, Home made Chinese, 114
Noodles, fried, Indonesian, 119
Noodles, Poppy seed, 124
Noodles, Velvet, 115

Omelette, Shredded, 74
Onion, Flan (Swiss), 44
Onion (or Soubise) purée, 43
Onion Rice, Swiss style, 78–9
Onion Soufflé, 55
Onions, Baby, in Sherry and Cream, 44
Onions with Beetroot, 27
Oriental Rice Case, 95

Paella, à la Valenciana, 79
Pasta, 97–8
Pasta, Californian salad, 112
Paste, Ravioli, 106–7
Paste, Vindaloo, 10
Pastry, quick puff, 17
Peanut Butter Sauce, *see* Chicken Satay
    with Peanut Butter Sauce, 69
Peanut Oil and Soya Sauce Dressing, 14
Peas with Shallots, 44
Pel'Meni in Broth, 114
Pel'Meni, Fried, 114
Pel'Meni, Russian, 113
Pel'Meni, Siberian, 114
Pel'Meni with Sour Cream, 114
Peppers, grilled, 45
Pie, Buckwheat and Mushroom, 89
Pie, Cauliflower, 34
Pie, Mushroom Lucerne, 43
Pie, Rice and Mushroom, 90
Pilaf, Mushroom, Uzbek Style, 77
Pilav, Turkish, 76
Pizzaiola Sauce, 14
Pont-Neuf Potatoes, or Chips French
    Style, 45
Poppy Seed Noodles, 124
Pork Fried, Indonesian, for Rijstafel, 73
Potato Croquettes, 47
Potato Purée, 46
Potatoes and Cabbage au Gratin,
    Austrian Style, 48
Potatoes, baked, 47
Potatoes Dauphinoise, 47
Potatoes, Duchess, 46–7
Potatoes, Jim Riley's Saratoga
    Creamed, 46
Potatoes, Matchstick, 45
Potatoes, Pont-Neuf, 45
Potatoes, Soufflé, 45

Potatoes, Straw, 45
Potatoes, Stuffed à la Campagnarde, 48
Prawn Sambal, 67
Preserved Duck Eggs, 70
Pudding, Noodle, Dalmatian, 123
Pudding, rice, baked, 95
Puff Pastry, quick, 17
Pulao, Bombay Cauliflower, 88
Purée, Potato, 46
Purée, Sorrel, 49–50
Purée Soubise, onion, 43

Quick Brioche Dough for Coulibiac, 17
Quick Puff Pastry, 17

Ramekins, Tetrazzini, 113
Ratatouille, 48
Ravioli, 106
Ravioli Filling, Cream cheese, 108
Ravioli Filling, Spinach, 108
Ravioli Filling, Spinach and Chicken,
    107
Ravioli Filling, Veal, 107
Ravioli Paste, 106–7
Red Beans à la Bourguignonne, 25–6
Red Cabbage, Flemish Style, 29–30
Regency Rice, 80
Rice, 56–8
Rice à la Cubana, White, 82
Rice à la Cubana, with eggs, 82
Rice à l'imperatrice, 94
Rice and Cabbage Soup, Italian, 60
Rice and Lobster Soufflé, 76
Rice and Mushroom Pie, 90
Rice and Spinach Timbale, 90–1
Rice, Basque, 80
Rice, Boiled Chinese (I), 61
Rice, Boiled Chinese (II), 61
Rice, Boiled Chinese (III), 61
Rice, Burmese Coconut, 75
Rice Cake, Oriental, 95
Rice, Cantonese and Steamed Chicken,
    62
Rice, Chinese with Mushrooms, 62
Rice Consommé, 59
Rice, Cream of, Soup, 59
Rice Croquettes, 75
Rice, Dessert, 93
Rice, Fisherman Style, 81
Rice Flans, 93
Rice Flan, Meringue, 94
Rice, fried, Hong Kong Style, 62
Rice, fried, Indonesian, 74
Rice Fritters, 94

Rice Gateau, 94

Rice, General notes on Rice Cooking in China, 56

Rice, General Notes on Rice Cooking in Japan, 57–8

Rice, Green—Risotto Verde, 84

Rice, Italian Soufflé, with Chicken Livers and Marsala, 86

Rice, Japanese Chestnut, 64

Rice Milan Style, Risotto alla Milanese, 83

Rice, Most Precious, 63

Rice Noodles Hong Kong Style, 116

Rice, Onion, Swiss Style, 78–9

Rice Pudding, baked, 95

Rice, Regency, 80

Rice Rings, 76

Rice, Rioja Style, 80

Rice Salads, 90

Rice, San Francisco Barbeque, 77

Rice Soufflé, Italian, 86

Rice, South Carolina, 78

Rice, Spring, 82

Rice with Fish, Punjab Style, 87

Rice with Four Cheeses, Riso a Quattro Formaggi, 87

Rice with Lobster Tendon, Tokyo Style, 63

Rice with Peas, Indian Style, 88

Rice with Tomato Sauce and Mayonnaise, 81

Rice, White, Cuban Style, 82

Rice, Wild, 91

Rice, Wild with Prawns, 91

Rigatoni, stuffed, 111

Rijstafel, 64–5

Rioja Rice, 80

Risotto alla Milanese, 83

Risotto alla Milanese with Marsala, 83

Risotto, Chicken and Gammon, 84

Risotto, sherried, 84

Risotto variations, 83

Risotto, Venetian, 83

Risotto Verde, green rice, 84

Russian Kasha or Rice and Salmon Culibiac, 89

Russian Pel'Meni, 113

Sajoer, 71

Salads, Rice, 90

Sambal, Bean, 66

Sambal, Chicken Liver, 66

Sambal, Fish, 65

Sambal, Prawn, 67

Sambal, Tomato, 65

San Francisco Barbecue Rice, 77

Sartù, 85

Satay, 68

Satay, Beef, 69

Satay, Chicken with Peanut Butter Sauce, 69

Satay Sauce (I), Without Oil, 14

Satay Sauce (II), With Oil, 14

Satay, Veal, 68

Sauce, Anchovy, *See* Spaghetti with Anchovy Sauce, 102

Sauce Avgolemono, Egg and Lemon, Greek, 10

Sauce Béchamel, 11

Sauce, Bolognese, 11

Sauce, Clam, for Spaghetti alle Vongole, 12

Sauce Cream, 12

Sauce Hollandaise, 12

Sauce Mayonnaise, 13

Sauce, Mornay, 13

Sauce Mousseline, 13

Sauce, Mushroom, 13

Sauce, Pizzaiola, 14

Sauce, Satay (I), Without Oil, 14

Sauce, Satay (II), With Oil, 14

Sauce, Tempura, 15

Sauce, Tomato, 15

Sauce, Tomato, Italian, 15

Sauce, Tunny, *See* Spaghetti with Tunny Sauce, 102

Sauce, Velouté, for Rice and Salmon Coulibiac, 15–16

Sauce Vinaigrette, 16

Sauce, White, 16

Sauerkraut à la Strasbourgeoise, 49

Savoury Noodle Pancakes, 121

Seroendeng, 67

Shao Mai, Pork and Prawn Steamed Dumplings, 119

Sherried Risotto, 84

Sherry Flavoured Spinach Mould, 51

Shredded Omelette, 74

Siberian Pel'Meni, 114

Sorrel Purée, 49–50

Soubise Purée, 43

Soto Ajam, Indonesian Chicken and Vermicelli, 72

Soufflé, Italian, Rice, with Chicken Livers and Marsala, 86

Soufflé, Onion, 55

Soufflé Pie, Carrot, 33

Soufflé Potatoes, 45

Soufflé, Rice and Lobster, 76
Soufflé, Rice, Italian, 86
Soufflé, Spinach, 54–5
Soufflé, Tagliatelle, 98–9
Soufflés, Vegetable, 54
Soup, Avgolemono, 59
Soup, Cream of Rice, 59
Soup, Rice and Cabbage, Italian, 60
Soup, Wun Tun, Chinese Ravioli, 118
South Carolina Rice, 78
Spaghetti Abruzzo Style, 104
Spaghetti Alla Carbonara, 104
Spaghetti Alle Vongole, 102
Spaghetti Umbrian Style, 104
Spaghetti with Anchovy Sauce, 102
Spaghetti with Oil and Garlic, 103
Spaghetti with Parsley Oil Sauce, 105
Spaghetti or Tagliatelle with Pesto, 103
Spaghetti with Tunny Sauce, 102
Spanish Cauliflower, 34
Spiced Eggs, 70
Spiced Fish Fillets, 70
Spinach and Chicken Filling for Ravioli, 107
Spinach and Mushroom Casserole, 51
Spinach Filling for Ravioli, 108
Spinach, Hong Kong, 50
Spinach, Sherry Flavoured Mould, 51
Spinach Soufflé, 54–5
Spinach Tarts, 50
Spring Rice, 82
Sprouts, Bacchanalian, 52
Straw Potatoes, 45
String Beans, Armenian Style, 27
Stuffed Cabbage Leaves, Russian Style, 30
Stuffed Cabbage with Olives and Rice, 29
Stuffed Mushrooms, 42
Stuffed Potatoes à la Campagnarde, 48
Stuffed Rigatoni, 111
Stuffed Tomatoes, 52
Stuffed Turnips, 53
Stuffed Vine leaves, 53
Sweetcorn, for Rijstafel, 71
Swiss Onion Flan, 44

Tagliarini with Chicken Livers, 100
Tagliatelle alla Bolognese, 98
Tagliatelle alla Crema, 99

Tagliatelle, Green, 98
Tagliatelle Soufflé, 99–100
Tagliatelle, or Spaghetti, with Pesto, 103
Tarts, Spinach, 50
Tempura Batter, 10
Tempura sauce, 15
Tetrazzini Ramekins, 113
Timbale, noodle, 120
Timbale, rice and spinach, 90–1
Tomato Fondue, 52
Tomato Sambal, 65
Tomato Sauce, 15
Tomato Sauce, Italian, 15
Tomatoes, Stuffed, 52
Tunny Sauce, *see* Spaghetti with Tunny Sauce, 102
Turkish Pilav, 76
Turnips, glazed, 53
Turnips, stuffed, 53

Ukrainian Vareniki, 123–4

Vareniki, Ukrainian, 123
Vareniki with Cherries, 124
Vareniki with Prunes, 124
Veal filling for Ravioli, 107
Veal Satay, 68
Vegetable Loaves, *see* Endive Loaf, 37
Vegetable Soufflés, 54
Vegetables stuffed with Soufflé Mixtures, 55
Velouté Sauce for Rice and Fish Coulibiac, 15–16
Velvet Noodles, 115
Venetian Risotto, 83
Vinaigrette sauce, 16
Vindaloo Paste, 10
Vine Leaves stuffed, Dolmathes, 53

White Beans with Butter, 25
White Rice à la Cubana, 82
White Sauce, 16
Wild Rice, 91
Wild Rice with Prawns, 91
Wun Tun, or noodle, paste, Chinese, 116
Wun Tun (Chinese Ravioli) Soup, 118

Zucchini, 40